前言 *PREFACE*

英国思想家培根说过：阅读使人深刻。阅读的真正目的是获取信息，开拓视野和陶冶情操。从语言学习的角度来说，学习语言若没有大量阅读就如隔靴搔痒，因为阅读中的语言是最丰富、最灵活、最具表现力、最符合生活情景的，同时读物中的情节、故事引人入胜，进而能充分调动读者的阅读兴趣，培养读者的文学修养，至此，语言的学习水到渠成。

"麦格希中英双语阅读文库"在世界范围内选材，涉及科普、社会文化、文学名著、传奇故事、成长励志等多个系列，充分满足英语学习者课外阅读之所需，在阅读中学习英语、提高能力。

◎难度适中

本套图书充分照顾读者的英语学习阶段和水平，从读者的阅读兴趣出发，以难易适中的英语语言为立足点，选材精心、编排合理。

◎精品荟萃

本套图书注重经典阅读与实用阅读并举。既包含国内外脍炙人口、耳熟能详的美文，又包含科普、人文、故事、励志类等多学科的精彩文章。

◎功能实用

本套图书充分体现了双语阅读的功能和优势，充分考虑到读者课外阅读的方便，超出核心词表的词汇均出现在使其意义明显的语境之中，并标注释义。

鉴于编者水平有限，凡不周之处，谬误之处，皆欢迎批评教正。

我们真心地希望本套图书承载的文化知识和英语阅读的策略对提高读者的英语著作欣赏水平和英语运用能力有所裨益。

丛书编委会

麦格希 **中英双语阅读文库**

科学普及系列

走进数理思维

第 *1* 辑

麦格希中英双语阅读文库编委会 ● 编

吉林出版集团股份有限公司

图书在版编目（CIP）数据

走进数理思维. 第1辑 / 美国麦格劳-希尔教育集团
主编；麦格希中英双语阅读文库编委会编；吴鹏，张娟
译. -- 2版. -- 长春：吉林出版集团股份有限公司，
2018.3
（麦格希中英双语阅读文库）
书名原文：Timed Readings Plus in Mathematics Book 1
ISBN 978-7-5581-4799-9

Ⅰ.①走… Ⅱ.①美… ②麦… ③吴… ④张… Ⅲ.
①英语—汉语—对照读物②数学—青少年读物 Ⅳ.
①H319.4：O

中国版本图书馆CIP数据核字(2018)第046099号

走进数理思维　第1辑

编：	麦格希中英双语阅读文库编委会	
插　画：	齐　航　李延霞	
责任编辑：	沈丽娟	
封面设计：	冯冯翼	
开　本：	660mm×960mm　1/16	
字　数：	225千字	
印　张：	10	
版　次：	2018年3月第2版	
印　次：	2018年3月第1次印刷	

出　版：吉林出版集团股份有限公司
发　行：吉林出版集团外语教育有限公司
地　址：长春市泰来街1825号
　　　　邮编：130011
电　话：总编办：0431-86012683
　　　　发行部：0431-86012767　0431-86012826(Fax)
印　刷：香河利华文化发展有限公司

ISBN 978-7-5581-4799-9　　定价：29.90元

Contents

1

Finding Your Car's Gas Mileage

How often will your family stop for gas while driving on a trip? If you know your *automobile*'s gas *mileage*, you can find the answer. Gas mileage is the total number of miles your car will travel on one *gallon* of gas. The farther you can travel on one *tank* of gas, the higher your gas mileage is.

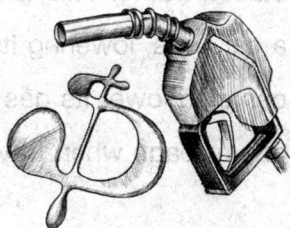

查明你汽车的里程油耗

你们一家人在旅行途中停车加油的频率是多少？如果你知道你家汽车的里程油耗，你就能找到答案。里程油耗指的是你的汽车消耗1加仑汽油所能行驶的英里数。用一箱汽油行驶的越远，里程油耗值就越高。

---

automobile *n.* 汽车
gallon *n.* 加仑

mileage *n.* 英里数；英里里程
tank *n.* 一箱（或一桶等）的量

Many factors can affect a car's gas mileage. Larger automobiles usually get lower gas mileage than smaller cars do because they are heavier and require larger *engines*. A large automobile filled with passengers will get even lower gas mileage. Small, fast sports cars with bigger engines tend to use more gas and have lower gas mileage than other small cars do.

How and where a car is driven affect gas mileage as well. City driving often involves lots of stopping and starting and sitting in stalled traffic. This kind of driving can increase the amount of gas a car uses, lowering its gas mileage. Driving a car up many tall hills can also lower its gas mileage. In most cases, cars will have higher gas mileage when traveling on highways and at a *steady* speed than

---

许多因素都可能影响汽车的里程油耗。相对小型汽车来说，大型汽车的里程油耗通常低于小型汽车的里程油耗，因为大型汽车更重一些，需要更大的引擎。坐满乘客的大型汽车，它的里程油耗会更低。带有较大引擎的小型赛车倾向于消耗更多的汽油，比其他小型车的里程油耗低。

汽车怎样行驶和驶去何地同样影响里程油耗。在交通阻塞的城市行驶时会有很多制动、启动和停车等待的动作。这种行驶方式可能会增加汽车的耗油量，降低它的里程油耗。开车爬很多陡坡也会降低它的里程油耗。大多数情况下，汽车在高速公路上匀速行驶比在城市的街道或山路上行驶时的里程油耗要高。定期做保养的汽车也会有更高的里程油耗，轮胎充气

---

engine *n.* 发动机；引擎　　　　　　　　steady *adj.* 匀速的；稳定的

when traveling on city streets or hilly roads. Cars that are regularly serviced get better gas mileage too. Cars with well-inflated tires get better mileage as well.

To *calculate* your car's gas mileage, you must know two things. First, how many gallons does your car's gas tank hold? Second, how many miles can your car travel on a full tank of gas? Your car's *odometer* shows how many miles the car has traveled. It is usually located near the *speedometer* on the car's *dashboard*.

Let's say your car's odometer reading was 8,450 miles when you last filled the tank, and it was 8,930 miles when the gas gauge was on empty. If you subtract 8,450 from 8,930, you find that your car traveled 480 miles on one tank of gas. Now let's say that the gas

---

量足的汽车同样会有更高的里程油耗。

为计算你家汽车的里程油耗，你必须弄清两个问题。第一，你家汽车的油箱里能装多少加仑汽油？第二，你家汽车加满油之后能行驶多少英里？你家汽车的里程表显示的是汽车已经行驶的英里数，它通常位于汽车仪表盘上速度计附近。

让我们假设在你上一次加满油后，你家汽车的里程表读数是8 450英里，当汽油计读数是0时，里程表读数是8 930英里。如果你拿8 930减去8 450，你得出汽车消耗一整箱汽油能行驶480英里。现在假设你的汽车的油箱能装20加仑汽油，那你现在就有了需要用来计算里程油耗的所有数

---

calculate v. 计算；核算　　　　　odometer n. 里程表；计程器
speedometer n. （车辆的）速度计　　dashboard n. （汽车上的）仪表盘

tank in your car holds 20 gallons of gas. You now have everything you need to find the gas mileage. *Divide* the 480 miles traveled by the 20 gallons of gas. Your car's gas mileage is 24 miles per gallon.

What if your car's gas tank holds 25 gallons of gas instead? The gas mileage would be lower. A trip of 480 miles divided by 25 gallons of gas is 19.2 miles per gallon.

据。用480英里除以20加仑汽油，得到你家汽车的里程油耗是24英里/加仑。

如果你家汽车的油箱容量是25加仑呢？那你家汽车的里程油耗就会降低。480英里的旅程除以25加仑汽油，里程油耗是19.2英里/加仑。

divide *v.* 除；除以

2

Choosing a New Car

Robert and Gosha want to buy a new car, but they cannot decide which kind of car to buy. "We need a car that's safe and also large enough for our growing family," Gosha says. "I'd like one that gets good gas mileage," Robert says. Both want a car that's *affordable*, one that doesn't cost too much money. They agree to choose

挑选一辆新车

罗伯特和寇莎想买一辆新汽车，但他们无法决定该买哪一种。"我们需要一辆安全性高且对于我们逐渐扩大的家庭来说足够使用的汽车，" 寇莎说。"我想买一辆里程油耗高的汽车，" 罗伯特说。他俩共同的要求是一辆支付得起，也就是不需要花费太多钱的汽车。最终他俩达成一致，在面包车和旅行车中选一种。

---

affordable *adj.* 付得起的；买得起的

between a *minivan* and a station wagon.

The next day, Robert and Gosha go to see their friend Sofia, who sells cars. "The station wagon costs $23,015," says Sofia. "It gets 19 miles per gallon in the city and 25 on the highway. The minivan is $27,245. It gets 16 miles per gallon in the city and 23 on the highway. The station wagon has a higher safety *rating*. Both can hold your large family, but the minivan has more room. We are offering a $3,000 *rebate* on the minivan." Sofia reminds them that a rebate is like a *refund*.

Robert and Gosha decide on the station wagon. "It costs $1,230 less than the minivan after the rebate. And it has a higher safety rating," says Gosha. "It doesn't have as much room as the minivan, but it does get a little better gas mileage."

　　第二天，罗伯特和寇莎去见他们一个销售汽车的朋友索非亚。"旅行车的售价是23 015美元。"索非亚说。"它在城市里的里程油耗是19英里/加仑，在高速公路上的里程油耗是25。面包车的售价是27 245美元，它在城市里的里程油耗是16，在高速公路上的里程油耗是23。相对于面包车来说，旅行车的安全等级更高。这两种车都能承载你们的大家庭，但是相对于旅行车来说，面包车有更多的空间。面包车现在可以打3 000美元的折扣。"索非亚提醒他们，3 000美元的折扣就像退款一样。
　　罗伯特和寇莎决定买一辆旅行车。"打折后旅行车的售价比面包车少1 230美元，而且它有更高的安全等级，"寇莎说。"它并没有和面包车一样多的空间，但是它有稍好一些的里程油耗。"

---

minivan *n.* 小型面包车；（八人）小客车

rebate *n.* 退还款；折扣

rating *n.* 等级；级别

refund *n.* 退款；返还款

3

Comparing Temperature Scales

How warm is it today? The answer to that question can be found by checking the temperature on an outdoor *thermometer*. Temperature can be measured using several kinds of *scales*. One is called the *Fahrenheit* scale, named after Daniel Fahrenheit, the man who invented it. Another is called the *Celsius*, or centigrade, scale.

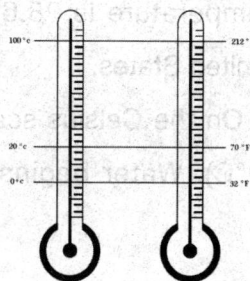

比较温标

今天气温有多少度？这个问题的答案可以通过使用室外温度计检测温度找到。温度能用多种温标表示。其中之一是华氏温标，是以华氏温标的发明者丹尼尔·华伦海特的名字命名的。另一个是摄氏温标或者说是摄氏度，百分度表示"100度"。摄氏温标是以其发明者安德斯·摄尔修斯的名字命名的。这两种温标都使用度或同等大小的其他单位

thermometer *n.* 温度计；寒暑表
Fahrenheit *adj.* 华氏温度计的；华氏的

scale *n.* 标度；刻度
Celsius *adj.* 摄氏的

Centigrade means "100 degrees." The Celsius scale was named after its inventor, Anders Celsius. Both scales use *degrees*, or steps of equal size, for measuring temperature. The two scales use very different methods, however.

A degree symbol (°) and the *abbreviation* for the temperature scale are often used to show temperature. On the Fahrenheit scale, the freezing point of water is 32 degrees Fahrenheit (32°F). The boiling point of water is *marked* at 212°F. The *normal* human body temperature is 98.6°F. The Fahrenheit scale is used only in the United States.

On the Celsius scale the freezing point of water is zero degrees (0°C). Water begins to boil at 100°C. The normal human body

---

来测量温度。然而，这两种温标的测温原理有很大区别。

度的符号"°"和温标的缩写常被用于表示温度。在华氏温标中，水的冰点是32华氏度（32°F），水的沸点记作212°F。人的正常体温是98.6°F，华氏温标仅用于美国。

在摄氏温标中，水的冰点是零度（0°C），水在100°C时开始沸腾。人的正常体温是37°C。摄氏温标在250年前最先在瑞典和法国使用，现在被广泛应用于各个国家。

---

degree *n.* 度；度数
mark *v.* 做记号；做标记

abbreviation *n.* 缩写形式；略语
normal *adj.* 正常的；一般的

temperature is 37°C. The Celsius scale was first used in Sweden and France almost 250 years ago. It is commonly used today.

The Kelvin temperature scale (K) was developed by Lord Kelvin in the mid-1800s. The zero point of this scale is equal to –273.15°C (–459.67°F). This zero point is the lowest possible temperature of anything in the *universe*. Therefore, the Kelvin scale is also known as the "*absolute* temperature scale." At the freezing point of water, the Kelvin scale reads 273.15K. At the boiling point of water, it reads 373.15K. The Kelvin scale is widely used by scientists, but it is *rarely* used in daily life.

Imagine it's a warm summer day and you see a sign that says the temperature is 25°C. How do you find the Fahrenheit temperature?

开氏温标是开尔文爵士于19世纪中期发明的。这个温标中的零点相当于-273.15℃（-459.67°F）。这个零点也是整个宇宙中可能出现的最低温度。因此，开氏温标也被称为"绝对温标"。在水的冰点处，开氏温标中记作273.15K。在水的沸点处，开氏温标中记作373.15K。开氏温标被科学家们广泛使用，但几乎不被用于日常生活中。

假想在一个温暖的夏日，你看见一个标志显示温度是25℃。那么你怎样才能知道对应的华氏温度是多少呢？你已知摄氏温标用100度从水的

---

universe *n.* 宇宙　　　　　　　　absolute *adj.* 绝对的；完全的
rarely *adv.* 很少；不常

You know that the Celsius scale uses 100 degrees to *span* the change between freezing and boiling. The Fahrenheit scale uses 180 degrees (32 through 212). You can find the relationship of Celsius degrees to Fahrenheit degrees by *multiplying* the Celsius *figure* by 1.8 (180 ÷ 100). Then add 32 degrees because the freezing point in Fahrenheit is 32 degrees higher than it is in Celsius. Your *computations*, then, are 25 × 1.8 = 45; 45 + 32 = 77. You have found that 25°C is the same as 77°F.

冰点跨越至沸点。华氏温标用180度来完成相应的跨越（从32到212）。你能通过将摄氏度数乘以1.8（180÷100）来找到摄氏温标和华氏温标之间的关系，再加上32度，因为华氏温标中的冰点比摄氏温标中的冰点高32度。那么你的计算结果是25×1.8=45；45+32=77。你就得出25℃相当于77°F。

---

span *v.* 持续；贯穿   multiply *v.* 乘；乘以
figure *n.* 数字   computation *n.* 计算；计算过程

4

Daniel Fahrenheit's Thermometer

Whether you are counting money or years, the number 100 is a common point for change. It would seem to be a *logical reading* on a temperature scale for the boiling point of water. Why, then, did Daniel Fahrenheit set the freezing point of water at 32 degrees and the boiling point at 212 degrees?

丹尼尔·华伦海特的温度计

无论你是在统计钱数还是年数，数字100都是一个常见的转折点。它似乎是一个基于温标的水的沸点的合乎逻辑的示数。那么，为什么丹尼尔·华伦海特将水的冰点设在32度，水的沸点设在212度呢？

logical *adj.* 符合逻辑的   reading *n.* （仪表的）读数

When Fahrenheit began his experiments in temperature, he used a *mixture* of salt and water. That mixture froze at a point he set as 0 on his scale. He decided to use temperature *intervals* of 12 degrees each. He may have used 12 instead of 10 because 12 is more easily divided by other whole numbers (2, 3, 4, 6). Fahrenheit went on to find that the normal body temperature could be *set* at the end of 8 of his 12-degree intervals (12 × 8 = 96), that is, at 96 degrees.

Fahrenheit *completed* his thermometer using the degree intervals he had set. He found that the boiling point of water was 212 degrees. Then he experimented with unsalted water. He found the freezing point of pure water to be at 32 degrees on his thermometer. Later it was found that his reading for body temperature was wrong. That reading was changed to 98.6 degrees.

当华伦海特开始他的温度实验时，他使用的是盐水混合物。他将这个混合物凝固时的温度设为他所建立的温标的零点。他设定每个温度的间隔是12度。他可能也用12来代替10，因为12更容易被其他整数（2，3，4，6）整除。华伦海特继续探明了人体正常体温可以设在以12度为一间隔的第八个间隔的末尾（12×8=96），就是96度。

华伦海特用他已建立的温度区间制成了华氏温度计。他发现水的沸点是212度。然后他用不含盐的水实验，发现纯水的冰点在他的温度计上显示的是32度。后来发现他的温度计上关于人的正常体温的示数是错误的。那个示数变成了98.6度。

---

mixture *n.* 混合物

set *v.* 设置；使处于

interval *n.* 间隔；间隙

complete *v.* 完成；结束

5

Percentages in Everyday Life

A percentage is a part of a whole. Percentages are *fractions* with the *denominator* 100. But instead of using the fraction 90/100, for example, we just use the *symbol* %, as in 90%. In fact, the word percent means "of 100." If you get 90 answers correct in an exam that has 100 questions, your score is 90 percent (90%).

日常生活中的百分率

百分比就是整体中的一部分。百分率是分母为100的分数。但我们只用百分号%，像90%，而不是使用分数90/100。事实上，单词percent的意思是"100分的"。如果在一次考试中有100道题，你答对了90道，那你的得分就是90分（90%）。

---

fraction *n.* 分数；小数　　　　　　　　denominator *n.* 分母
symbol *n.* 符号；记号

Imagine you need to wash 40 windows. After a while, you see that you've finished eight of them. What percentage have you completed? To *figure* percentage, you begin with the numbers you know and make a *comparison* to 100. Therefore, you would figure that eight windows is to 40 windows as X percent is to 100 percent. To find the number X, work with the known numbers. First multiply 8 times 100, which is 800. Then divide 800 by the other known number (40). You've washed 20 percent of the windows.

Shopping for almost any product often involves percentages. For example, the *label* on a department store *blouse* may be marked as "65% cotton, 35% silk". Food labels and packages show the percentage of the recommended daily amount of proteins, vitamins,

---

假设你需要清洗40扇窗户，过了一段时间以后，你发现你已经清洗完了其中的8扇。那你已经完成的百分比是多少呢？为计算百分比，你首先用你已知的数字计算再与100作一个对比。然后，你就计算8扇窗户比40扇窗户等于X%比上100%。为解出X，对已知数据进行计算，首先用100乘以8，得800。接着用800除以另一个已知数字（40）。结果是你已经清洗了这些窗户中的20%。

购买几乎任何产品通常都会涉及百分率。例如，一件百货公司的衬衫的标签上可能标记 "65%棉，35%丝"。食品的标签和包装纸上显示建议每天摄入的蛋白质、维他命和其他由食物提供的基础营养物质的百分比。

---

figure *v.* 计算　　　　　　　　　　　　comparison *n.* 比较；对照
label *n.* 标签；签条

and other basic elements provided by the food. Many soda and water bottles are made from a percentage of *recycled* plastic goods, just as many paper products contain a percentage of recycled paper.

Let's say that you and your friends decide to go to the mall. You have the money you made from washing windows. You find a leather coat that is marked 30 percent off the regular price. The original price was $90. You need to know how much money you would save if you buy this coat. Begin with the known numbers. The savings is 30 percent. Think of the *formula* as 30 percent is to 100 percent as X dollars is to 90 dollars. First multiply the known numbers (30 × 90), which comes to 2,700. Then divide this product by 100. The difference is 27. Your savings is $27. When you subtract this amount from $90, the sale price is $63.

很多苏打水和纯净水瓶都是由含有一定百分比的回收塑料的材料制成的，就像许多纸质产品里含一定百分比的回收废纸一样。

让我们假设你和你的朋友打算去商场购物。你有一笔擦窗户赚来的钱。你找到一件皮革上衣，上面标着"降价30%"，原价是90美元。你需要知道如果你买了这件衣服可以节省多少钱。从已知数据开始：可节省的钱是30%，考虑等式：30%比上100%等于X美元比上90美元。首先将已知数据相乘（30×90），结果是2 700。再用这个得数除以100。商是27。那你节省的钱就是27美元。当你从90美元中减去这部分时，售价就是63美元。

---

recycle *v.* 回收利用；再利用　　　　　　formula *n.* 计算式；公式

The store *charges* sales tax on purchases. This tax is a percentage too. If the tax is 6 percent on your $63 *purchase*, your tax is $3.78 (6 × $63 = $378, and $378 ÷ 100 = $3.78).

Later, you and your friends go to a restaurant. The bill for three sandwiches is $14.40. Your friends turn to you to calculate the 15 percent tip. No problem, right?

商店要对顾客所购商品支付销售税。这个税额也是一个百分数。如果税收是你所购买的63美元商品的价格的6%，那你这件衣服的税就是3.78美元（6×63美元=378美元，378美元÷100=3.78美元）。

随后，你和你的朋友们去了餐厅。购买三份三明治，账单上是14.4美元。你的朋友们向你求助，计算15%的小费是多少。你肯定没问题，对不对？

---

charge *v.* 收费；（向……）要价   purchase *n.* 购买；购买的东西

6

Levon's Challenge

At the end of the last school year, Levon and his dad took an *extended* look at Levon's test scores. Levon knew how to calculate an average for a set of numbers: Add the figures together, and then divide the *sum* by the number of figures that were added.

Levon had scored 73, 87, 80, and 84

莱文面临的挑战

在上一学年末，莱文和他的爸爸对莱文的考试分数进行了进一步考察分析。莱文学会了怎样计算一系列数字的平均数：将所有数字相加，再拿和除以所有相加数字的个数。

在四次数学考试中，莱文的得分分别为73、87、80、84。这四次分数的总和是324。那么，他的数学平均分就是81分（324除以4）。在四次

---

extended *adj.* 延长了的；扩展了的   sum *n.* 和；总数

percent on four math tests. The sum of the four test scores added together was 324. His *average*, then, was 81 percent (324 divided by 4). His scores on four English tests were 88, 80, 86, and 82 percent. The sum of the four test scores added together was 336. So his average was 84 percent. Levon's social studies and science test averages were 92 and 71 percent.

Next they wanted to know the average of all the test scores. Levon had taken the same number of tests in each *subject*, so they added the math, English, social studies, and science test averages together and divided by 4. The average of all his test scores last year was 82 percent.

They could see that the science test scores were bringing down the total test score average. Levon's father offered a deal to his son. "Raise your average test scores," he said, "and I will raise your *allowance*."

英语考试中，莱文的得分分别为88、80、86、82。这四次分数的总和是336。他的英语平均分就是84分。莱文的社会研究和科学的平均分分别是92分和71分。

接下来他们想知道所有分数的平均数。莱文每门科目的考试次数是相同的，所以他们将数学、英语、社会研究和科学考试平均分加起来，再除以4。得出他去年所有考试的平均分是82分。

他们会发现科学考试分数降低了所有考试的总平均分。莱文的爸爸提供给儿子一个方案。他说，"如果下学期你的平均分提高了，我将会给你更多的零用钱。"

---

average *n.* 平均数　　　　　　　　　　subject *n.* 科目；学科
allowance *n.* 零用钱

7

Using a Road Map

Maps are interesting as well as useful. Most maps are *representations* of Earth's surface. Mapmakers show the relationship between the distances on the map and real distances on Earth by providing a map scale. This relationship is expressed as a *ratio*. A map of a town might have a ratio of 1:100,000. This means that

路线图的使用

地图既有趣又实用。绝大多数地图是对地球表面各个区域的描画。地图制作者通过提供比例尺来表明图上距离和实际距离之间的关系。这个关系是用比例表示的。一张城镇地图可能会用1：100 000这个比例。这意味着地图上的1英尺等于地球上的100 000英尺。当你知道1英里有63 360英尺时，你就会明白100 000英尺等于多少英里了。100

---

representation *n.* 描述；描绘　　　　　　ratio *n.* 比率；比例

one inch on the map equals 100,000 inches on Earth. You can find how many miles 100,000 inches are when you know that there are 63,360 inches in a mile. So 100,000 ÷ 63,360 = 1.58 miles. In other words, one inch on the map represents 1.58 miles on Earth.

There are small-scale maps and large-scale maps. A small-scale map shows a large area with a small amount of detail. A large-scale map shows a small area with a large amount of detail. One way to understand this is to imagine you are *floating* in a balloon just above your hometown. As you look down, the ratio of the area you see might be expressed as 1:10,000. As the balloon rises, the details become smaller, and the scale also becomes smaller. An example of

---

000÷63 360=1.58英里。换句话说，地图上的1英尺代表地球上的1.58英里。

　　有小比例尺地图和大比例尺地图。一个小比例尺地图表现的是一个大区域及其中的小部分细节。一个大比例尺地图表现的是一个小区域及其中的大部分细节。能用来理解这些图的一种方法是想象你在一个漂浮在你家乡上空的气球里。当你向下看时，你所看到的区域的比例尺可能就用1：10 000来表示。当气球逐渐上升时，细节部分就逐渐缩小，比例也就随之变小了。一张比例尺为1：1 000 000的地图就是一个小比例地图的例子。

---

float *v.* 浮；漂浮

a small-scale map is a map with the ratio 1:1,000,000.

Road maps, like many other maps, show the distance in miles between places. Road maps are large-scale maps. However, road maps usually do not show the large-number ratio of one inch to thousands or hundreds of thousands of inches. They often show only the smaller ratio, one inch to miles.

Now let's use a map scale on a road map to find out the distance from your home to the state *capital*. You find your town and the capital on the map and see that a single direct road connects them. The scale shows that 1 inch = 25 miles. *Measuring* the distance on the map between your town and the capital, you find they are seven

---

像其他的地图一样，路线图表示不同地方之间的距离（英里）。路线图是大比例地图。然而，路线图通常不显示诸如1英尺：几千或成千上万英尺的大比例。它们通常只显示小比例，1英尺：多少英里。

现在让我们用路线图上的比例尺来计算你家与州首府之间的距离。你首先在路线图上找到你所居住的城镇和州首府，发现这两地之间有一条直通的路连接着。比例尺表明1英尺=25英里。在地图上测量你所居住的城镇和首府之间的距离，你得出它们之间隔着7英尺。那么，州首府距离你家175英里。

---

capital *n.* 首都；首府   measure *v.* 测量；度量

inches apart. The state capital, then, is 175 miles from your home.

Along the way is Centerville, a little less than two inches from your town, or about 40 miles away. You have to pick up a new soccer *jersey* there. To calculate the amount of time it takes to travel to Centerville, you need to know your travel speed as well as the number of miles you need to travel. The speed limit is 55 miles per hour. If you travel at that speed, you should be in Centerville in about 45 minutes.

　　从你居住的城镇出发，沿着这条路走路略少于2英尺或大约40英里就到了森特维尔。你必须在那里去拿一件新的足球运动套衫。为计算去森特维尔所要花费的时间，你必须了解你的行驶速度和你需要行驶的英里数。速度上限是每小时55英里。如果你以这个速度行驶，你应该需要大约45分钟的时间到达森特维尔。

---

jersey *n.* 参赛者运动衫

8

Are We There Yet?

Kim and Hector wanted to visit friends across the state. Kim purchased a road map to help them find the shortest *route* and to *figure out* how many miles they had to travel.

Hector remembered a trip he had taken to Aurora State Park. He had gotten there by the shortest route he could find on his

我们到了吗?

金和赫克托尔想去拜访整个州上的朋友们。金买了一张路线图来协助他们找到最短路径并计算出他们必须要行驶多少英里。

赫克托尔还记得他的极光国家公园之旅。他用能在路线图上找出的最短路径到达了目的地。但很多路段的速度上限都很低。他的总行驶时间比

---

route *n.* 路线;路途　　　　　figure out 计算(数量或成本)

map. But many of the roads had low speed limits. His total travel time was almost two hours longer than he thought it would be. Going home, he took a route that was 25 miles longer on the map, but his trip was almost an hour shorter.

Along with their map, Hector and Kim decided to use a mileage *chart* to plan their trip across the state. A mileage chart shows the shortest distance between selected cities. Kim made a list of the cities they would pass through along their way. Next, Hector found the distance from their starting point to the first city along the route. Then he found the distance from that city to the next one on the route. Finally, he added all of the distances together. They now knew the shortest route and the total number of miles to their destination.

他预期的差不多长了两个小时。返家的过程中，他采取了在地图上比之前路径长25英里的路线，但他的返程时间比来的时候少了近一个小时。

依照路线图，金和赫克托尔决定用航程图来规划他们遍及整个州的行程。航程图会显示你所选择的城市间的最短距离。金将他们沿途中会经过的城市列了一个清单。接下来，赫克托尔找出他们沿途中会经过的第一个城市与起点之间的距离。然后他找出路线图上从这个城市到下一个路过的城市之间的距离。最后，他将所有的距离值加在一起。现在他们知道到达他们的目的地的最短路径和整个里程数。

---

chart *n.* 图表

9

Shopping for the Best Value

Careful *grocery* shoppers may have difficulty making a "quick trip" to the market. They often need to take time finding the best value for their money. They wonder whether they should buy the large *can* or the small can. They think about which product tastes better. If you're

采购物美价廉的商品

对于那些细心的食品采购者来说，在市场上快速完成采购可能是有困难的。他们通常需要花时间思考怎样才能让钱花得最值。他们想知道是应该买大宗商品还是小宗商品才能最合算。他们还要考虑哪

---

grocery *n.* 食品杂货；食品杂货店   can *n.* 一听（的量）；金属罐

looking for the best value, you need to compare *items*. To compare means to look at how one item measures up against others.

When you compare prices, be sure that the quantity, or amount of each item, is the same. If the quantity is different, you might not choose the best value. Items such as milk and orange juice are sold in various units of measure. Gallons, *quarts*, *pints*, and *ounces* are four of the most common units of measure. Each pint holds 16 ounces. Each quart holds two pints. And each gallon holds four quarts. When comparing items of different quantities, you must consider the price per unit of measure.

种产品味道最好。如果你想让钱花得最值，你就需要对商品进行比较。作比较就意味着针对商品的某一项测量指标值进行比较，以挑选产品。

当你比较价格时，你要确保每个商品的数量是一样的。如果是在数量不同的情况下作比较的，你可能就挑不到最物美价廉的商品了。诸如牛奶、橙汁类的物品常以各种度量单位出售。加仑、夸脱、品脱、盎司是四种最常见的度量单位。1品脱相当于16盎司，1夸脱相当于2品脱。1加仑相当于4夸脱。比较不同量的物品时，你必须考虑单位含量的物品的价格。

---

item *n.* 一件商品（或物品）

pint *n.* 品脱

quart *n.* 夸脱

ounce *n.* 盎司

For example, milk is often sold in gallons, half gallons, and quarts. A gallon of White Star milk costs $2.99. A half gallon costs $1.79. And a quart costs $1.19. Which is the better value? At first it may seem that the quart and half gallon are better values because they are cheaper than the gallon. To compare prices, however, remember to compare the same *amount* of each product. Two *individual* quarts of milk cost $2.38($1.19 × 2). That means the half gallon is a better value than the two quarts. Two half gallons of milk, which equal one full gallon, cost $3.58 ($1.79 × 2). The gallon of milk at $2.99 is cheaper by $0.59. Usually, larger quantities are cheaper per unit than smaller quantities.

例如，牛奶通常以加仑、1/2加仑、夸脱出售。1加仑白星牛奶售价是2.99美元。1/2加仑白星牛奶售价是1.79美元。1夸脱白星牛奶售价是1.19美元。哪一种比较划算呢？乍一看似乎是夸脱和1/2加仑比较划算，因为它们的售价低一些。然而，为比较价格，要记住比较相同数量的产品。2夸脱牛奶的总价钱是2.38美元（1.19×2=2.38美元）。这意味着1/2加仑比2夸脱划算。两个1/2加仑的牛奶，相当于1加仑，花费3.58美元（1.79×2=3.58美元）。那1加仑2.99美元的产品就比两个1/2加仑的便宜0.59美元。一般说来，较大数量物品的单位价格低于较小数量物品的单位价格。

---

amount *n.* 数量；数额　　　　　　individual *adj.* 单独的；个别的

So should you always buy the largest quantity of an item? If your family cannot drink a gallon of milk in a week, the milk may *spoil*. In *cases* like this, buying the smaller quantity at a higher price per unit may be the better choice. You may feel that Blue Circle milk tastes better than White Star milk. However, a gallon of Blue Circle milk costs $3.69. You might buy Blue Circle because, for you, that is a better value. Buying the largest quantity or the cheapest *brand* may not always be the best choice. When you consider all of your choices, you can make the best decision about the value of a product.

　　那你是否应该一直买最大数量的商品呢？如果你们一家人一周内喝不完1加仑牛奶，剩下的就坏掉了。这种情况下，购买那些量少一些、单位价格高一些的产品是比较好的选择。你可能会觉得蓝圈牛奶的口感比白星牛奶好。但是，1加仑蓝圈牛奶的售价是3.69美元。你可以购买蓝圈牛奶，因为对于你来说，它就是最合算的。购买最大数量或是最廉价类型的产品可能不会一直是最佳选择。当你认真思考过你所有可能的选择后，你就能作出最佳选择，买到最合算的产品。

---

spoil *v.* 变质；变坏　　　　　　　　　　case *n.* 具体情况；特殊情况
brand *n.* 类型；品牌

10

Comparing Breakfast Cereals

Rudy wanted to buy a healthful *cereal* for his children. He also needed to find the best value for the money. He chose rice, *bran*, and wheat with *raisins* for his comparison.

"The rice cereal has the highest amount of vitamin A but less *calcium* than the other two," Rudy thought. "The wheat with

比较谷类早餐

鲁迪想为他的孩子们买一种健康谷物。他也需要让他的钱花得值得。他选择大米、麦麸、混有葡萄干的小麦作比较。

"大米中维他命A含量最高，但是钙含量比其他两者低，"鲁迪想。"混有葡萄干的小麦中其他种类维他命的含量都是最高的。"鲁迪继续比较。大米中含有3%的建议食用的膳食纤维。麦麸中的膳食纤维含量是大

---

cereal *n.* 谷物；谷类食物
raisin *n.* 葡萄干

bran *n.* 糠；麦麸
calcium *n.* 钙

raisins has the highest amount of all other vitamins." He continued comparing. The rice cereal has 3 percent of the *recommended* daily amount of *fiber*. The bran has four times as much fiber (12 percent), but the wheat with raisins cereal has more than six times as much (20 percent).

The wheat with raisins cereal comes in a 24-ounce box and costs $4.79. The bran cereal is in an 18-ounce box for $4.29. The rice cereal, in an 18-ounce box, is the least expensive at $2.88. That means the wheat with raisins cereal is 20 cents per ounce (4.79 divided by 24). The bran cereal is 24 cents an ounce (4.29 divided by 18). And the rice cereal is 16 cents an ounce (2.88 divided by 18).

"I'll buy two boxes of wheat with raisins cereal," Rudy thought. "It's not the cheapest, but it has the highest vitamin *content*."

米中的4倍，就是12%，而混有葡萄干的小麦中膳食纤维含量比大米中的6倍还要多，20%。

一盒24盎司的混有葡萄干的小麦要花费4.79美元。一盒18盎司的麦麸要花费4.29美元。而一盒18盎司的大米是三者中最便宜的，2.88美元。这意味着1盎司混有葡萄干的小麦要花费20美分（4.79÷24），1盎司麦麸要花费24美分（4.29÷18），1盎司大米要花费16美分（2.88÷18）。

"我要购买两盒混有葡萄干的小麦，"鲁迪想。"它不是最便宜的，但维他命含量是最高的。"

---

recommend *v.* 推荐；建议   fiber *n.* （食物中的）纤维素
content *n.* 含量；容量

11

Catering an Event

People who want to host a social event, such as a sales meeting or a birthday party, sometimes *hire caterers* to provide food and services. Caterers are businesses that prepare and serve food for events. Some caterers also provide music, gifts, and *decorations*.

为活动供应膳食

当人们想要举办一场社交活动，例如销售会议、生日宴会，有时会雇用酒席承办商提供食物和服务。酒席承办商就是为活动准备和提供食物的职业。有一些酒席承办商也提供音乐、礼物和装饰等服务。

---

hire *v.* 雇用
decoration *n.* 装饰品

caterer *n.* 饮食服务公司；酒席承办商

Caterers need to ask several questions to learn what services are needed. How many guests will attend the event? What kind of food should be served, and how much food will be needed? Will the guests be served from a *buffet*, or will waiters serve the food at the guests' tables? What sort of *beverages* will be served?

People who hire caterers usually decide on a *budget*, or a plan to use a certain amount of money, for the entire event. To do this, they must find out what the caterer charges for the items they want. Then they must plan carefully and make *adjustments* so that the total cost fits within the budget.

In this example, Apex Wrenches wants to *host* a *conference* and hire Candy's Catering to serve lunch. The guests will be 250 new

---

酒席承办商需要问一些问题以了解雇主需要什么样的服务。有多少宾客参加这个活动？需要提供什么种类的食物？需要多少量？是通过自助餐的方式来招待客人，还是侍者在餐桌旁为客人服务？需要提供什么种类的饮料？

雇用酒席承办商的人通常凭借预算或计划来决定为整个活动花费一定数额的钱。为了做这些，他们必须查明他们所需服务项目的收费情况。然后他们必须仔细地计划并适当调整以保证整个花费不超过预算。

在这个例子中，阿派克斯扳手公司打算举办一场会议，并雇用坎迪餐馆提供午餐。宾客是250名新销售人员。阿派克斯还想让坎迪餐馆提供小

---

buffet *n.* 自助餐

budget *n.* 预算

beverage *n.* （除水以外的）饮料

adjustment *n.* 调整；调节

salespeople. Apex also wants Candy's to provide small key chain *wrenches* as gifts to each of the lunch guests. Apex sets the budget for the event at $5,000(250 × $20).

Candy's charges $20 a person for lunch, so the meals will cost $5,000. There will be no money left for the gifts, which cost $300. Apex and Candy's must work together to make a few changes in the plans. Candy's tells Apex that the charge for a buffet-style lunch is only $12 a person, or a total of $3,000 (250 × $12). The cost is less because Candy's would not have to pay as many waiters to serve lunch. Apex agrees to the change and learns that Candy's charges an *additional* $5 a person for a selection of desserts, or a total of $1,250 (250 × $5). Apex adds the desserts to the menu because the

---

型钥匙链扳手作为礼物赠送给每位到场的客人。阿派克斯为这次活动做的预算是5000美元（250×20美元）。

坎迪的餐馆对每位客人的午餐收费是20美元，因此午餐的费用将是5000美元。这样一来将没有剩余的钱来为每位客人买礼物，买礼物需要300美元。阿派克斯和坎迪餐馆必须合作，在原计划中做一些改动。坎迪餐馆的人员告诉阿派克斯，如果提供自助餐式的午餐，每位客人只收取12美元，总额是3000美元（250×12美元）。这种情况下花费少的原因是坎迪餐馆将不需要支付许多为午餐服务的侍者的钱。阿派克斯赞同这项改动并了解到坎迪餐馆为提供一系列甜品要对每位客人收取额外的5美元，

---

host *v.* 主办；主持（活动）
wrench *n.* 扳钳；扳手

conference *n.* 会议；讨论会
additional *adj.* 附加的；额外的

total cost of the desserts, the buffet, and the gifts comes to $4,550. There is $450 left in the budget.

Candy's has to think about its budget too. It has to buy the food and purchase special *containers* to carry it to the event. Candy's also has to buy and *maintain* vans to *deliver* the food. Cooks must be paid to make the food, and waiters must be hired to serve the food. Candy's figures out how much of these costs can be added to the price of its services.

总额是1 250美元（250×5美元）。阿派克斯将甜品加到菜单中，因为甜品、自助餐和礼物的总额才4 550美元，预算中还有450美元的余额。

坎迪餐馆也必须考虑预算。餐馆需要采购食物并购买特殊容器将食物带到活动现场。坎迪餐馆也要购买和保养运货车以便派送食物。要支付厨师的薪金，还要雇用提供食物的侍者。坎迪餐馆要计算出有多少诸如此类的花费能被加到餐饮服务费里。

---

container *n.* 容器　　　　　　　　　　　　　maintain *v.* 维修；保养
deliver *v.* 运载；传送

12

Rachel's Bat Mitzvah: The Costs and Arrangements

Rachel's 12th birthday is coming up soon. She'll celebrate her bat mitzvah, an important *rite* in a Jewish girl's life. Many Jewish girls celebrate their bat mitzvah with traditional *prayers* and *practices*. And often there is also a celebration party!

瑞秋的成人礼：成本和安排

瑞秋的十二岁生日就要到了。她将庆祝她的成人礼，这在犹太女孩的一生中是一个很重要的仪式。很多犹太女孩以传统的祈祷和习俗来庆祝她们的成人礼。通常还会有一个庆祝宴会。

---

rite *n.* （宗教等的）仪式；典礼　　prayer *n.* 祷告；祈祷仪式
practice *n.* 习惯；习俗

Rachel's parents have planned to spend $1,000 on the bat mitzvah, the same amount they spent on her older brother's bar mitzvah. The party will be held in the family's *backyard*.

Her mother has ordered two *fancy* sheet cakes, enough for 100 people. Rachel will honor her mother, grandmothers, and aunts by lighting candles on the cakes. The cakes cost $100 each. For entertainment, Rachel's cousins will play traditional dance music. They will be paid $250. The family has *arranged* to spend $400 on food and beverages.

Rachel found a beautiful party dress for $125, but buying it would leave only $25 for some decorations she really wants. Then Rachel's mother discovered that they had forgotten to add in the cost of

---

瑞秋的爸妈已经计划好花1 000美元在这个成人礼上，这和过去在瑞秋哥哥的成人礼上花费的数额是一样的。宴会将在瑞秋家的后院里举行。

瑞秋的妈妈已经预订了两款精致的单层大块蛋糕，足够100个人享用。瑞秋将在蛋糕上点燃蜡烛来对她的妈妈、奶奶还有阿姨表示敬意。这些蛋糕100美元一个。为了娱乐，瑞秋的表兄妹们将演奏传统舞曲。他们将被支付250美元。瑞秋家已经安排好花费400美元在食物和饮料上。

瑞秋发现了一件漂亮的礼服，需要125美元，但是如果买了这件礼服，就只剩下25美元来做她特别渴望的舞会现场装饰了。此外瑞秋的妈妈发现他们之前忘记把盘、叉、刀、汤匙等餐具费加到预算中。现在有三种

---

backyard *n.* 后院；屋后附属地带   fancy *adj.* 精致的；高档的
arrange *v.* 安排；筹备

plates, forks, knives, and spoons. There are three choices. Rachel's parents can *contribute* more money to the amount they had set aside for the party. Or they can cut back and have less music or food or fewer guests. Or Rachel can buy a less expensive dress.

方案。瑞秋的父母能拿出更多的钱来支付他们之前没考虑到的部分。要么他们可以削减开支，少一些音乐表演或少提供一些食物或少请一些客人。要么瑞秋可以买一件便宜一点的礼服。

---

contribute *v.* 增加；添加

13

Small-World Theory

Each year Ben is glad when Martin Luther King Jr. Day gives him a day off from school. Ben knows that this day *honors* an important man, but Ben doesn't feel connected to him. In a sense, however, Ben really is linked to Dr. King through the "small-world theory." Ben's mom (0) has a *stepfather* (1) whose uncle (2) once met and

小世界理论

每一年马丁·路德·金日学校都会放假一天，本很开心。本知道这一天是为了纪念一个重要的人物，但本并没有感受到与这位伟大的人物之间存在联系。然而，在某种意义上来说，本是通过"小世界理论"与金博士联系到一起的。本的妈妈有一个继父，这位继父的叔叔曾经遇到埃莉诺·蒙代尔并和她交谈过，埃莉诺·蒙代尔是前副总统沃尔

---

honor *v.* 尊敬；尊重   stepfather *n.* 继父

spoke to Eleanor Mondale (3),the daughter of *former* Vice President Walter Mondale (4), who knew Dr. King (5). In a way, Ben is only "five people away" from Martin Luther King Jr.

The small-world theory says that everyone in the world is connected through a short *chain* of people they know. This chain is known as degrees of *separation*. There are zero degrees of separation between you and the people you know directly. So there are zero degrees between Ben and his mom. There is one degree of separation when just one person separates you from someone you don't know. So Ben's mom's stepfather is one degree away from Ben. As the chain continues, the stepfather's uncle is two degrees, Eleanor Mondale is three degrees, her father is four degrees, and Dr. King is five degrees away from Ben. The theory goes on to say that

---

特·蒙代尔的女儿，沃尔特·蒙代尔认识金博士。某种意义上说来，本与马丁·路德·金仅仅只有"五个人的距离"。

小世界理论称世界上的每一个人都是通过他们所认识的人组成的短链联系起来的。这个链也被称为分离度。你和你直接接触的人之间就是0度分离。所以本和她的妈妈之间就是0度。当仅有一个人将你和你不认识的人隔离开时，就是1度分离。所以本的妈妈的继父和本的距离就是1度。随着链的持续，继父的叔叔就是2度，埃莉诺·蒙代尔就是3度，她的父亲沃尔特·蒙代尔是4度，金博士和本之间就是5度分离。这个理论还认为世界上任意两个人之间都不会有六度以上的分离。

---

former *adj.* 以前的；昔日的
separation *n.* 分离；分开

chain *n.* 锁链；链条

there are no more than six degrees of separation between any two people in the world.

The small-world *theory* is *based* on math. The theory *assumes* that a person knows 100 people and that each one of those people knows 50 different people. Each of those 50 people knows another 50 people, and so on. If the calculation is *carried out* to six degrees, it multiplies as follows: $100×50×50×50×50×50=31.25×10^9$, or more than 31 billion. The world has about 6 billion people. So in theory, six degrees of separation can cover the world.

Does the small-world theory work? It has never been proved. There are questions about how well it can *apply* in some areas. For example, the theory needs to *establish* links to *remote* groups of

---

小世界理论是建立在数学基础之上的。这个理论假定一个人认识100个人，这100个人中，每位认识50个不同的人，这50个不同的人里的每一个又认识另外的50个人，以此类推。当计算六度分离时，计算过程如下：$100×50×50×50×50×50=31.25×10^9$，或者说是多于310亿。这个世界上有大约60亿人口。因此在这个理论中，六度分离就能够遍及全世界了。

那么小世界理论可用吗？这个理论一直没有得到证实。对于它如何能很好地应用在一些领域，还存在一些问题。例如，小世界理论需要在关系较远的人群之间建立联系。因此，在那些只认识同村里的人，几乎不认识

---

theory *n.* 理论；原理
assume *v.* 假设；假定

based *adj.* 以（某事）为基础的；为根据的
carry out 执行；实施

people. So it may not work in faraway places where everyone knows the people in their village but few know anyone outside it. Also, the theory relies on a few people with huge *networks* who link the rest of us.

Does the theory matter? Maybe it just makes us all think a little more about our place in the world.

村子外的人的边远山区里，这个理论可能就不适用了。还有，小世界理论依赖小部分拥有巨大社交网络的人将剩下的人们联系在一起。

那么小世界理论重要吗？也许它仅仅是让我们所有的人对我们周围的世界多一点思考。

---

apply *v.* 应用；使用　　　　　　establish *v.* 建立；确立
remote *adj.* 关系较远的；遥远的　　network *n.* 网络；关系网

14

What Is Chance?

One day Kelly picked up the phone to call Lynn, and there was no *dial tone*. Then Kelly heard Lynn say, "Hello?" "Lynn?" Kelly said. "I was just going to call you!"

A mysterious *coincidence*? Not really. The laws of *probability account for* this happening.

Kelly and Lynn call each other two or three times a day, or about 1,000 times a

什么是可能性？

一天，凯莉拿起电话，打给林恩，没有听到拨号音。接着凯莉就听到林恩说，"喂？""是林恩吗？"凯莉说。"我刚才正要给你打电话呢！"

这难道是一个不可思议的巧合吗？不见得。概率法则能解释这一现象。

凯莉和林恩每天相互打两或三次电话，或者说是每年大约一千次。我

---

dial tone 拨号音
probability *n.* 概率；几率

coincidence *n.* 巧合；巧事
account for sth 解释；说明

year. Let's say that the *variable* N stands for the total number of calls that the two friends make to each other in a year. Now, for purposes of example, let's say that the *chance* of their calling each other at the same moment is 1 in 1,000 (.001). Let's call that number p. The laws of chance say that Np (N×p) equals the average number of times in a year that they are likely to call each other at the same moment. So if Kelly and Lynn call each other 1,000 times in a year, 1,000×.001 equals one call a year. It was *mathematically* likely to happen sometime.

People calculate *odds* for fun. A famous example is called the "birthday problem." It states that in any group of 23 people, there's a 50-50 chance that two of them will share a birthday.

们假设变量N代表一年中这两个朋友间相互打电话的总次数。为了举例，我们假设他们俩在同一时间给对方打电话的可能性是1/1 000（0.001）。我们把这个称为P，概率原理指出：NP（N×P）相当于一年中他们可能在同一时间给对方打电话的平均次数。因此，如果凯莉和林恩在一年中互相打1 000次电话，1 000×0.001相当于一年打一次。基于数学原理来说，可能会发生。

人们有时会为娱乐而计算概率。一个很著名的例子叫做"生日问题"。它这样说道，在任意一个23人的群体中，他们其中的两个在同一天过生日的可能性是1/2。

---

variable *n.* 变量；可变因素　　　　　　chance *n.* 可能性
mathematically *adv.* 数学上　　　　　　odds *n.* 可能性；几率

15

Race Cars—Behind the Speed

Race cars are some of the fastest-moving machines in the world. An Indystyle *race* car, the kind that races at the Indianapolis 500, can reach speeds above 230 miles per hour. That's faster than many small planes travel when they take off and fly.

赛车——速度背后的秘密

赛车是世界上移动最快的机械。一辆印度风格的赛车，在印第安纳波利斯500比赛中，最高时速能达到230英里。这个速度要高于一些小型飞机在刚起飞时的速度。

race *n.* 赛跑；速度竞赛

Since race cars change direction often, race teams are interested in a car's *velocity* as well as its *speed*. Velocity is the rate at which something moves in a certain direction. *Whereas* speed also tells us how fast something moves, it tells us nothing about the object's change of position. Distance divided by time equals speed. *For instance*, if you drive 140 miles in two hours, moving westward, your speed is 70 miles per hour (140÷2=70 mph). However, your velocity is 70 mph west.

Let's say that Jenny drove at 70 miles per hour to the next town and then returned home at the same speed. On average, her speed was 70 mph, but her average velocity was 0, because overall she

---

　　由于赛车经常改变方向，因此赛车队对赛车的速率和速度都很感兴趣。速度是当一个物体沿某一确定方向运动时的速度。尽管速率也表示的是物体运动的快慢，但不考虑运动过程中方向是否改变。路程除以时间就是速率。例如，如果你在两小时内向西行驶140英里，你的速率是每小时70英里（140÷2=70英里/小时）。但是，你的速度却是70英里/小时，向西。

　　我们假设珍妮以70英里/小时的速率行驶到邻城，接着再以相同的速率返回。那她的平均速率就是70英里/小时，但她的平均速度就是0英里/

---

velocity *n.* （沿某一方向的）速度　　　　speed *n.* （运动的）速度；速率
whereas *conj.* 然而；但是；尽管　　　　for instance 例如；比如

did not change her position—she came back to the very point where she started.

One factor that can lower a car's speed and velocity is *friction*. Friction is a force that slows down *motion*. As a race car moves, its rolling tires *rub* against the track, causing friction.

When engineers design race cars, they study the *coefficient* of friction. This involves considering both the weight of an object and the force needed to move that object. For instance, a 100-pound box may require 20 pounds of force to push it across a floor. To compute the coefficient of friction, the engineer would divide 20 by 100, getting a result of 0.2. Objects such as oiled machine parts and

---

小时，因为最终她并没有改变她的位置，全程结束时，她又回到了最初出发的位置上。

能降低汽车的速率和速度的因素之一就是摩擦力。摩擦力是一种能减慢物体移动的力。当赛车移动时，滚动的轮胎就会与赛轨之间产生摩擦，因而有了摩擦力。

当工程师设计赛车时，他们会认真研究摩擦系数。这包括考虑物体的重量和移动物体所需要的力的大小。例如，一个重100磅的箱子可能需要20磅的力推动它通过地板。为计算摩擦系数，工程师会用20除以100，

---

friction *n.* 摩擦；摩擦力
rub *v.* 摩擦

motion *n.* 运动；移动
coefficient *n.* 系数

race car wheels have a much lower coefficient of friction—usually about 0.002.

The science of *aerodynamics* studies the ways that air friction affects the motion of objects. As a race car passes through air, *forces* push against it. People who design race cars study these forces to improve the *performance* of their cars. Drag is a kind of force produced by air friction that slows the car down. Downward forces help hold the car on the track. The more force holding a car on the track, the faster it can go around corners and through *curves*. So, designers of race cars try to reduce the car's drag while increasing the downward forces.

得到结果0.2。像油机零件、赛车轮等物体的摩擦系数要低得多，通常在0.002左右。

空气动力学研究大气摩擦是如何影响物体运动的。当一辆赛车在空气中穿过时，大气摩擦会产生相反方向的阻碍力。设计赛车的人研究这些力以提高其设计的赛车的性能。牵引力是由大气摩擦产生的减慢车速的阻力。向下的力有助于保持汽车在赛道上。维持赛车在赛道上的力越大，车子在拐角和拐弯处行驶的速度就越快。因此，赛车的设计者尽力降低赛车的牵引力但同时提高赛车的下向力。

---

aerodynamics *n.* 空气动力学　　　　　force *n.* 力
performance *n.* 性能；表现　　　　　curve *n.* 弯曲处；拐弯处

16

Horsepower

Horsepower is a *unit* of measure that tells you the power of an engine. *Horsepower* was first used as a unit of measure in the late 18th century by James Watt. Watt built a *steam* engine that was more powerful than the earlier steam engines. He compared the power of his steam engines to the power of his horses.

马 力

马力是一个表示引擎功率的测量单位。在18世纪末期，马力首先被詹姆斯·瓦特用作测量单位。瓦特发明了一个比之前使用的蒸汽机功率大很多的蒸汽机。他把他发明的蒸汽机的功率和他的马的功率作比较。衡量物体做功的快慢——物体能被移动的最快速度叫做功率。将

---

unit *n.* 单位；单元　　　　　　　　　horsepower *n.* 马力（功率单位）
steam *n.* 水蒸气；蒸汽（动力）

The measure of the rate of doing work—how fast something can be moved—is called power. The amount of work needed to move one pound of matter the distance of one foot is a foot-pound. A single horsepower equals 550 foot-pounds per second. Three horsepower equals 1,650 foot-pounds per second.

The horsepower of a *vehicle* engine is not the same as the horsepower driving the vehicle's wheels. A *massive truck* and a small car might both have a 190-horsepower engine. However, the weight of the truck could mean a loss of 20 percent of its horsepower. The horsepower turning the truck's wheels is only 152 (190 hp × 20% = 38; 190 − 38 = 152). The lightweight car may lose only 10 percent of its horsepower. Its wheels get a higher amount (190 hp × 10% = 19; 190 − 19 = 171).

1磅物体移动1英尺距离所需要做的功就是英尺磅。1马力相当于550英尺磅/秒。3马力相当于1650英尺磅/秒。

　　车用发动机的额定马力与实际驱动车轮的马力是不相等的。一辆大型卡车和一辆小汽车可能都有一个190马力的引擎。然而，卡车的重量可能意味着20%的马力损耗。驱动卡车车轮的马力仅有152（190马力×20%=38；190-38=152）。轻型的汽车可能只损失10%的马力。它的轮子就得到更大一部分马力（190×10%=19；190-19=171）。

---

vehicle *n.* 交通工具；车辆
truck *n.* 卡车；载重汽车

massive *adj.* 巨大的；大而重的

17

Roman Numerals

The Roman number system was developed by the ancient Romans. Unlike the ancient Greeks, the Romans did not develop theories requiring the use of numbers, such as in *geometry* and *physics*. The Romans used their numbers mainly for doing business. Roman *numerals* were used for keeping records of taxes and trade

罗马数字

罗马数字是由古罗马人发明的。不同于古希腊人的是，古罗马人并没有建立需要使用数字的理论，例如几何学和物理学。古罗马人的数字主要用在做生意中。罗马数字曾在整个大罗马帝国史上被用来记录税收和贸易。

---

geometry *n.* 几何学
numeral *n.* 数字；数码

physics *n.* 物理学

throughout Rome's great *empire*.

The Romans used numerals that are the same as some of our letters. The numerals I, V, X, L, C, D, and M *stand for* 1, 5, 10, 50, 100, 500, and 1,000. For a large number, the single number *values* are arranged from left to right, beginning with the greatest value and ending with the smallest value. The value of the *entire* number is then found by adding all of the single number values together. The number MDCLXVI, for example, would be read as 1,000 + 500 + 100 + 50 + 10 + 5 + 1, or 1,666.

Some numbers include the same letter more than once. The number 8 is VIII, formed by adding three ones to V. If numbers with lower values are to the right of a larger number, the lower numbers are added to the larger number. So, the number VIII is 5+1+1+1=8.

　　古罗马人使用的数字中，有一些和我们的部分英语字母是相同的。数字I，V，X，L，C，D和 M 分别代表1，5，10，50，100，500，1 000。对于一个比较大的数字，将单个数字从左到右排列，从数值最大的开始排起，以最小的那个结束。组合数字的值是通过将所有单个数字的值相加得到的。例如，数字MDCLXVI会被看成1 000+500+100+50+10+5+1，或者是1 666。

　　有一些数字中同一个字母会出现不止一次。数字8用罗马数字表示是Ⅷ，是由一个 v 加三个 I 组成的。如果一些值低的数字放在值高的数字右边，小数字就加到大数字中。所以，数字Ⅷ就是5+1+1+1=8。

---

empire *n.* 帝国
value *n.* 值；数值

stand for 是……意思；代表
entire *adj.* 全部的

Except for very large numbers, Romans never used the same numeral more than three times in a row. Instead of writing the number 4 as IIII, subtraction is used. The rule is: If a number with a lower value is to the left of the larger number, then the lower number is subtracted from the larger number. Four is 5 minus 1, or IV. Nine is 10 minus 1, or IX. Forty is 50 minus 10, or XL.

The subtraction *feature* of Roman numerals may make figuring out the value of some three-letter numbers *puzzling*. For example, XIX is 19, or 10 + 9. Why isn't XIX 21, or 10 + 1 + 10? Simply stated, the subtraction rule means that IX stands for 9. XIX is therefore 10 (X) plus the smaller number, 9 (IX), that follows, or 19. The numeral for 21 is XXI.

除了一些非常大的数字以外，古罗马人从不在同一行中使用同一个数字三次以上。数字4是用减法方式表示的，而不是用 IIII 。规则是：如果低值数字在高值数字的左边，那么就用高值数字减去低值数字。4等于5减1，即IV。9等于10减1，即IX。40等于50减10，即XL。

罗马数字的减法特征可能导致一些三字母数字的值的计算让人迷惑。例如，XIX是数字19，或者是10+9。那XIX为什么不是21，或者说是10+1+10呢？简而言之，减法规则意味着IX代表9。因此XIX就是10(X)加上较小的数字，9(IX)，也就是19。罗马数字中表示21的是XXI。

---

feature *n.* 特征；特点   puzzling *adj.* 令人费解的；迷惑的

Roman numerals are still used today, but not very often. Roman numerals are often seen *carved* into a corner of some large buildings to show when the buildings were constructed. Roman numerals are also seen on the faces of clocks and watches and in the first pages of books.

罗马数字在今天仍然被使用，但不是很常用。在一些大型建筑物的建设过程中，罗马数字通常被刻在这些大型建筑物的拐角处来表示建造的时间。在时钟、手表的表盘里和书的扉页上也能看到罗马数字。

carve *v.* 刻；雕刻

18

The Arabic Numerals and Place-Value

The Arabic numerals 0, 1, 2, 3, 4, 5, 6, 7, 8, and 9 in use today are a clear, easy-to-use set of symbols for *counting*. The Arabic numerals are based on a number system first used in *ancient* India. The Arabic number system was the first to use the zero. Before this system, the idea of zero was sometimes shown by using

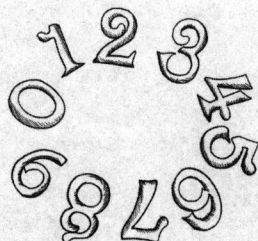

阿拉伯数字和位值

我们现在使用的阿拉伯数字0，1，2，3，4，5，6，7，8和9是一组清晰的、易于使用的计数符号。阿拉伯数字序列最早是在古印度使用的数字序列的基础上建立起来的。在这套数字序列出现以前，有时候用空白来表示0的意思。然而，用这种方法处理，经常会造成混

---

count *v.* （按顺序）数数；计算总数　　　　　　　ancient *adj.* 古代的

a blank space. This way of doing things, however, often caused confusion. Blank spaces might be forgotten when writing a number or missed when reading a number.

Perhaps the most important feature of Arabic numerals is place-value. Each of the numbers 1 to 9 *occupies* a single place. Then, once 10 is reached, a second place is begun with 1 and then 0 from left to right. These positions *remain* the same as we count through 99. At 100, a third place is begun with 1 - 0 - 0 from left to right. These positions remain the same until 999 is reached. Beginning with 1,000, four spaces are used, as 1 - 0 - 0 - 0 fill those spaces from left to right. The practice of place-value helped simplify the process of addition and subtraction as well as *multiplication* and *division*.

淆。空白可能在写数字的时候被忘记或是在读的时候被漏掉。

也许阿拉伯数字最重要的特征就是位值。数字1到9中的每一个都占据一个个位。接着，当满10时，第二位从1开始，然后0位从左至右。这些位置在我们数到99以前都是等同的。到100时，三位数从1-0-0开始，从左向右。这些位置在我们数到999以前都是等同的。从1 000开始，要使用4位了，从1 000开始，从左到右依次填补每一位。采用位值的处理方法促进了加法、减法、乘法和除法运算过程的简化。

---

occupy *v.* 使用；占用　　　　remain *v.* 仍然是；保持不变
multiplication *n.* 乘；相乘　　division *n.* 除（法）

19

Consumers and Lenders:
The Business of Borrowing Money

People who want to buy an expensive item such as a car will likely need to get a *loan*. When a *consumer* wants to buy a house, the long-term loan the buyer will need is called a *mortgage*. Banks will lend money to people who have paid their bills on time and established good *credit*. Lenders decide whether they want to lend

借贷者和贷款人：信贷行业

那些想要购买像汽车这样昂贵商品的人可能需要获得一些贷款。当一个消费者想要买一套房子时，买家可能需要的长期贷款叫做抵押贷款。银行会将钱借给那些已经按期还清债务并建立了良好信誉度的人。贷款方通过检查客户的信用历史来决定是否愿意借钱给客户。这是

---

loan *n.* 贷款；借款　　　　　　consumer *n.* 消费者；顾客
mortgage *n.* 按揭；按揭（或抵押）贷款　　credit *n.* （借钱偿还的）信誉；信用

a customer money by examining the customer's credit history. This is a record of how much money a person *owes* and how *promptly* that person has been paying his or her bills.

A lender will also want to know how much a borrower *earns* each month. This will help the bank decide whether the borrower would be able to repay a loan. For instance, a customer applies for a car loan. The person's monthly take-home pay is $1,200. The customer has monthly credit card payments of $175 and monthly *rent* payments of $500. That means there is $525 left over for other monthly expenses. The bank needs to decide whether the customer can afford a $260 car payment each month.

Banks and other lenders such as mortgage companies make a profit from lending money. They make money by charging people

---

关于一个人曾负债多少，又是花费多长时间还清债务的记录。

贷款方也会想要知道借款人每个月的收入是多少。这将会帮助银行判断借款人是否有能力还款。例如，一个客户申请一项汽车贷款，这个人每个月的税后薪水是1 200美元。这个客户每月要为信用卡支付175美元，为房租支付500美元。这意味着剩下525美元供每月其他方面的花费。银行需要判断这名客户是否能负担每月260美元的车贷。

银行和其他像贷款公司这样的贷款方通过借款给他人来赚取利润。他们通过向借贷者收取利息来赚钱。他们收取的这部分利息也叫做利率。利

---

owe *v.* 欠债；欠账
earn *v.* 挣钱；赚得

promptly *adj.* 及时地；迅速地
rent *n.* 租金

interest. The amount of interest they charge is called the interest rate. It is a percentage of the loan amount. For example, a customer who gets a $10,000 loan with a 7 percent interest rate will need to pay back a total of $10,700 to the lender. Some banks offer lower interest rates than others. They might do this especially with customers who have strong credit reports. That is because banks believe that people with good credit are more likely to *repay* a loan than people with poor credit. It is a good idea to look around for the best interest rate *available*. On a three-year car loan of $10,000, for example, a 7 percent interest rate means a monthly payment about $18 higher than with a 3 percent interest rate.

Banks and other companies that lend money borrow from the Federal Reserve Bank, which decides the rate of interest it will

率是贷款总额的一个百分比。例如，一个获得利率为7%的10 000美元贷款的客户将需要还款总共10 700美元给贷款方。一些银行提供相对其他贷款方来说低利率的贷款，特别是针对那些信誉度等级很高的客户。这是因为，银行认为有良好信誉的客户偿还贷款的可能性比那些信誉度差的客户要大得多。对于借贷者来说，多作调查，寻找可得到的最佳利率是个好主意。例如，对于一个总额为10 000美元的三年购车贷款，7%的利率相对于3%的利率来说，意味着每个月要多支付18美元。

　　银行和其他一些公司将从美国联邦储备银行借来的钱再转借给他们的

interest *n.* 利息　　　　　　　　　　　　　　　　repay *v.* 归还；偿还
available *adj.* 可获得的；可找到的

charge other banks. This is called the *prime rate*. It affects the amount of interest the banks charge. How much a person will have to pay to borrow money depends on three major factors. These are the prime rate, the person's credit history, and competition among lenders.

客户，这就决定了它收取其他银行的利率。这个利率也叫做最优惠贷款利率。最优惠贷款利率影响银行收取的利息数额。一个人为贷款所支付的费用取决于三个主要因素。它们分别是最优惠贷款利率、个人的信用历史、贷款方之间的竞争。

prime rate　（美国银行的）最优惠贷款利率

20

The Terms of a Home Mortgage

There are two common types of mortgage loans. A loan with a *variable*, or *adjustable*, *rate* has an interest rate that may change from year to year. A fixed-rate mortgage loan has an interest rate that stays the same for the entire *term* of the mortgage.

房屋抵押贷款的相关条款

有两种常见的抵押贷款。可变利率或可调利率的抵押贷款，利率可能逐年改变。固定利率的抵押贷款，在整个抵押期内，利率都保持不变。

variable *adj.* 可更改的；可变的
rate *n.* 比率；率

adjustable *adj.* 可调整的；可调节的
term *n.* 期；期限

Mortgages most often have a term of 15 or 30 years. During this time, monthly payments are made on the loan. For a 30-year mortgage, repayment is *spread out* in 360 payments (12 months × 30 years = 360). In most cases, one would pay less each month on a 30-year mortgage than on a 15-year loan. However, the borrower must pay interest for 30 years. Most banks and mortgage companies offer customers a lower interest rate on a loan with a shorter term.

On a 15-year, *fixed-rate* home mortgage of $100,000 with an interest rate of 5 percent, the monthly payment would be $790.79. Over 15 years, the borrower would pay $42,342.86 in interest.

抵押贷款最常见的年限是15年或者30年。在这期间，根据贷款数额分月偿还。对于一个30年期限的抵押贷款，偿还被分成360次支付（12月×30年=360）。在大多数情况下，一个人每月为30年期限抵押贷款支付的钱要少于为15年抵押贷款支付的钱。然而，30年期限抵押贷款的借贷者需要支付30年的利息。大多数银行和借贷公司向他们的客户提供短期的低利率的贷款。

对于一个15年期限的固定利率为5%的100 000美元房屋抵押贷款，每个月的支付额将是790.79美元。15年后，借贷者将支付42 342.86美元的利息。

---

spread out 分（若干次）进行

fixed-rate *adj.* 固定利率的

Maybe the borrower purchased a home with a 30-year, fixed-rate loan of $100,000 and an interest rate of 5.75 percent. The *monthly* payment in this case would be only $583.57. However, over 30 years, the borrower would pay $110,086.23 in interest.

也许借贷者通过一个30年期限的固定利率为5.75%贷款的100 000美元购买了一套房子。在这种情况下，每个月的支付额将仅有583.57美元。然而，30年后，借贷者将支付110 086.23美元的利息。

---

monthly *adj.* 每月一次的；按月的

21

How Did Our Calendar Develop?

The *calendar* most often used today is called a *solar* calendar. Solar means "having to do with the sun." The solar calendar is based on the time it takes Earth to travel once around the sun. Earth makes this journey around the sun in 365¼ days. Our calendar has 365 days every three out of four years. To make up for the *extra* one-

我们的日历是怎么发展起来的?

今天我们最常使用的日历叫做阳历。单词"solar"的意思是"与太阳有关的"。阳历是基于地球绕太阳转动一圈的时间建立的。地球完成绕太阳一圈的旅行需要365.25天。我们使用的日历,每四年中有三年是365天的,为了处理多余的1/4天,每四年中有一年是366天。

---

calendar *n.* 日历;挂历   solar *adj.* 太阳的
extra *adj.* 额外的;外加的

quarter day, it has 366 days every fourth year. The four one-quarter days are joined into one day and added to the fourth year, called a *leap year*. The extra day in a leap year is the 29th day in February.

The solar calendar is not the only way of counting the months. People in earlier times based their calendars on the cycle of the moon. Their months started with the new moon and lasted about 29 days. Calendars based on the moon are called *lunar* calendars. Lunar calendars are still used.

The solar calendar can be *traced back to* ancient Rome, about 2,000 years ago. The first Roman calendar had been based on the cycles of the moon. It lasted 304 days and was divided into 10 months, for an average of 30.4 days per month. Then the Roman emperor Julius

---

四个1/4天凑在一起就是完整的一天，加到第四年里，叫做闰年。闰年里多出来的一天是2月29日。

阳历并不是计算月份的唯一方式。古时候人们基于月亮周期来制作日历。他们的月份从新月开始，持续约29天。基于月亮的日历叫做阴历。阴历至今仍被使用。

阳历的由来可追溯至古罗马时期，大约2 000年以前。第一个罗马日历是基于月亮的周期建立起来的。它持续304天，被分成10个月，每个月平均30.4天。后来罗马皇帝凯撒到埃及旅行，在那里他了解到埃及人是怎

---

leap year 闰年

trace (back) (to sth) 追溯；追究

lunar *adj.* 月球的；月亮的

Caesar made a trip to Egypt, where he learned how the Egyptians measured time. When Caesar returned to Rome, he changed the calendar. Instead of a lunar calendar with 304 days divided into 10 months, he *created* a 12-month solar calendar with 365 days every three out of four years and a leap year every fourth year.

In 1582 Pope Gregory XIII, with the help of his scientists, made more changes to the solar calendar. It became the calendar that we use today. This calendar became known as the Gregorian calendar. Like the calendar that Caesar created, the Gregorian calendar set the year at 365 days, with a leap year every fourth year. The Gregorian calendar *worked* better than Caesar's calendar and other earlier calendars. But it was not fully accepted until the 20th century.

样计量时间的。当凯撒返回罗马后，他就更改了日历。他创造了阳历计日，每年12个月，每四年中有3年是365天，每四年出现一个闰年，代替了之前持续304天、分成10个月的阴历计日。

1582年，教皇格里高利十三世在他的科学家的帮助下，对阳历作了更多的改动。这就变成了我们今天使用的阳历，这个日历也被称作格里高利历。像凯撒制定的日历一样，格里高利历也将一年定为365天，每四年出现一个闰年。格里高利历比凯撒制定的及之前的日历更有效。但它直到20世纪才被完全接受。

create *v.* 创造；创作　　　　work *v.* 奏效；产生……作用

Keeping track of the number of days in each month of our solar calendar can be a *challenge*. Many years ago, the following *rhyme* was created to help us remember how many days are in each month:

Thirty days have September,

April, June, and November.

All the rest have thirty-one,

Except February the only one

Which leap years change each fourth time

From twenty-eight to twenty-nine.

要了解我们使用的阳历中每个月的天数是个难题。很多年以前，人们创作了下列押韵诗来帮助我们记住每个月的天数：

4月，6月，9月，11月有30天。

其余的都有31天，

除了2月这一个，

它在闰年时变化，每四年一次

从28天变至29天。

---

keep track of sth 了解   challenge *n.* 挑战；艰巨任务

rhyme *n.* 押韵的短诗

22

The Chinese Calendar

The Chinese calendar shares features of both the solar and lunar calendars. It is called a "lunisolar" calendar. The Chinese calendar is usually made up of 12 months. Each month *corresponds* to the *phases* of the lunar cycle. The solar year is 12 months and about $365\frac{1}{4}$ days. The lunar cycle is completed in about $29\frac{1}{2}$ days. So, a

中国日历

中国日历同时具有阳历和阴历的特征。它被称为"阴阳历"。中国日历通常由12个月组成。每个月和月亮周期的各个阶段相对应。阳历年有12个月，大约365.25天。一个完整的月亮周期大约是29.5天。因此，12个月的阴历年将会有12×29.5=354天，或者说是比阳历年

---

correspond *v.* 相一致；符合   phase *n.* 时期；月相

12-month lunar year will be about 12 × 29.5 = 354 days, or about 11 days shorter than a solar year.

A leap month is added about every third year to keep the Chinese calendar *in tune with* the seasons. A complete *cycle* of this calendar takes 60 years. This period is divided into five cycles of 12 years each.

The Chinese calendar is used for setting the dates of traditional festivals, such as the Chinese New Year. The Chinese New Year begins on the first day of the Chinese calendar and lasts for 15 days. The Chinese New Year celebrates the beginning of spring. The beginning of the Chinese year always falls between January 21 and February 21 on the Gregorian calendar.

少了约11天。

每三年要有一个闰月加进去，以保持中国日历和季节的一致。这种日历的一个完整周期要经历60年。这一周期被分为五个循环，每一个循环是12年。

中国日历被用作确定像中国新年这样的传统节日的日期。中国的新年从中国日历的第一天开始并持续15天。中国新年是为庆祝春节，即新的一年的到来。中国新年的开端通常位于格里高利历的1月21日到2月21日之间。

---

in tune with （与……）协调；一致　　　　cycle *n.* 循环

23

The Pyramids of Egypt

The Great Pyramid is called one of the Seven Wonders of the Ancient World. It was built for the *pharaoh* Khufu, a leader of the Egyptian people. He was *buried* in a room at the heart of the *pyramid*. The stones of the room fit together so well that a card could not pass between them. The Great Pyramid is more than 4,500

埃及金字塔

"大金字塔"被称为古代世界的七大奇迹之一。它是为古埃及人民的领袖——法老胡夫建立的墓地。他被埋在位于金字塔中心的一个房间里。这个房间的石墙结合得如此紧密以至于连一张卡片也穿不过去。大金字塔已有超过4 500年的历史了。它在古代世界的

---

pharaoh *n.* 法老（古埃及国王）

pyramid *n.* 金字塔

bury *v.* 埋葬；安葬

years old. It is the oldest of the Seven Wonders and the only one that still stands.

To build the Great Pyramid, the Egyptians needed to measure a square *base*, with four right angles. The pyramid's base has been found to be level within a *margin* of 2.1 centimeters, less than 1 inch. The base covers about 13 *acres* and is 751 feet long on each side. The four corners of the base point exactly to the north, south, east, and west.

More than 2.3 million blocks were carved from *limestone* and granite and then pulled, pushed, and dragged for miles to the building site. The average weight of each block was about 2.5 tons, or about 5,000 pounds. Some of the blocks weighed as much as 16 tons, or 32,000 pounds. It took the Egyptians about 20 years to complete the Great Pyramid.

七大奇迹中是年代最久远的，也是唯一一个至今仍然存在的古建筑。

为建造大金字塔，古埃及人需要测量一个呈正方形，并有四个直角的底面。金字塔的底面误差水平已被算出，在2.1厘米左右，少于1英寸。底面覆盖约13英亩，每边长751英尺。底面的四个拐角正对着北、南、东、西四个方向。

超过230万块由石灰石和花岗岩凿出的石块，通过拉、推和拖动数英里至建筑工地。每块石头的平均重量约为2.5吨，或者约5 000磅。一些石块的重量重达16吨，或者说是32 000磅。古埃及人民花费了近20年的时间才建成大金字塔。

---

base *n.* 基底；底座
acre *n.* 英亩

margin *n.* 差额；差数
limestone *n.* 石灰岩

A major problem facing the builders of the Great Pyramid was getting the large stone blocks into place. Most people agree on the method the Egyptians used to achieve this. It is believed that they built *ramps* laid upon *inclined planes* made of brick and *rubble*. The ramps were slicked with water and mud. The workers would then push and drag the blocks up the slippery ramps. Eventually, as the pyramid grew taller, the ramps, and the inclined planes that supported the ramps, had to be made longer. The base of the inclined plane had to be widened also, or else it would have collapsed under the great weight.

The Great Pyramid was 481 feet high when it was finished. The Egyptians themselves had no tools for measuring the height of the pyramid. The Greek mathematician Thales, while visiting at the time, showed the Egyptians how to measure the height of a pyramid. He

---

大金字塔建造者面临的主要问题之一就是如何将大型石块运送至工地。大多数人就古埃及人采用何种方法完成这项任务这一问题持相同的观点。一种普遍的观点是：他们在由砖和碎石组成的斜面上建了斜坡。在斜坡表面铺了水泥浆，以使其变光滑。然后工匠会推、拖石块到滑坡道上。最终，金字塔越筑越高，斜坡、支撑斜坡的斜面就必须不断加长。斜面的基础也必须加宽，否则它就会不堪重负而倒塌。

大金字塔竣工时高481英尺。古埃及人自己没有可用的工具来测量金字塔的高度。希腊数学家泰雷兹当时正巧在那里旅行，就向古埃及人演示了怎样测量金字塔的高度。他在金字塔旁等待一天中他的影子长度和身高

---

ramp *n.* 斜坡；坡道   inclined *adj.* 倾斜的；成某角度的

plane *n.* 平面   rubble *n.* 碎石；碎砖

waited for the time of day when his shadow's *length* equaled his own height. From his knowledge of mathematics, Thales knew that at this same moment, the length of the pyramid's shadow must also equal the pyramid's height. So Thales simply measured the pyramid's shadow.

相等的时刻，因为泰雷兹知道在这一刻，金字塔的影子长度也一定和它自身的高度相等。因此，泰雷兹仅需要测量金字塔的影子的长度，就能得出金字塔的高度。

---

mathematician *n.* 数学家　　　　　　　　　　　　length *n.* 长；长度

24

Measuring the Surface Area of a Pyramid

A pyramid such as the Great Pyramid in Egypt is a *three-dimensional solid*. The base is a *polygon*, and the sides are *triangles* that meet at a point called the apex. The surface area of a pyramid is the sum of the area of the base and all the sides. How would we measure the surface

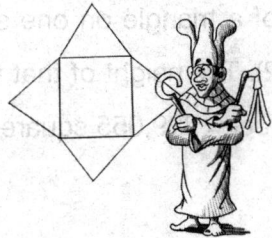

测量金字塔的表面积

像埃及大金字塔这样的锥形塔是三维立体结构的。它的底面是一个多边形，侧面是一些三角形，所有侧面相交的那一点叫做顶点。金字塔的表面积就是底面和所有侧面的面积之和。那我们怎样才能测量出大金字塔的表面积呢？我们已知它的底面是一个正方形，因为它有四个直角，底面的每一边长度都是751英尺。因此，我们可以用正方形面积

---

three-dimensional *adj.* 三维的　　　　　solid *n.* 固体；立体图形
polygon *n.* 多边形；多角形　　　　　　triangle *n.* 三角形；三角形物体

area of the Great Pyramid? We know that its base is a square because it has four right angles. Each side of the base measures 751 feet in length. So, we can use the formula for finding the area of a *square*: length (751 feet) × width (751 feet) = 564,001 square feet.

How do we find the area of the four sides? You'll have to picture in your mind the Great Pyramid. The sides of a pyramid with a square base are *identical* triangles. The formula for finding the area of a triangle is one-half of the base multiplied by the height. Half the base of a triangle on one side of the Great Pyramid is 375.5 feet (751 ÷ 2). The height of that triangle is about 610 feet. So, 375.5 feet × 610 feet = 229,055 square feet.

公式来计算：长（751英尺）×宽（751英尺）=564 001平方英尺。

那我们怎样计算四个侧面的面积呢？你必须在你脑海中描绘出大金字塔的样子。底面是正方形的大金字塔，侧面是4个全等的三角形。三角形的面积计算公式是底边的一半乘以高。大金字塔的一个侧面三角形的底边的一半是375.5英尺（751÷2）。这个三角形的高大约是610英尺。因此，375.5英尺×610英尺=229 055平方英尺。

square *n.* 正方形；四方形　　　　　　　identical *adj.* 相同的；同一的

Finally, add the area of the base (564,001 square feet) to the sum of the areas of all sides (229,055 square feet × 4), and the surface area is 1,480,221 square feet.

The surface area of the Great Pyramid today is less than it was when it was new, because the rock *face* has been worn down by the weather.

最后，把底面的面积（564 001平方英尺）加到所有侧面积的和（229 055平方英尺×4）中，得出大金字塔的表面积是1 480 221平方英尺。

现如今大金字塔的表面积比当初刚建成的时候要小，因为岩石的表面已被风化了。

---

face *n.* （某物的）面；表面

25

Measuring Circles

Geometry is a *branch* of mathematics that studies points, lines, planes, and figures, including circles. Everywhere you look, you can see examples of circles.

All points on a circle are the same distance from the center of the circle. In other words, a true circle is perfectly round. You can draw a line from the center of a

测 圆

几何是研究点、线、面和包括圆形在内的几何图形的学科，是数学的一个分支。生活中到处都能看到有关圆形的例子。

圆上所有的点到圆心的距离都是相同的。换言之，一个标准的圆完全是圆的。你可以从圆心画一条到圆上任一点的线。圆心到那点的距离叫做

---

branch *n.* （学科及语言的）分支

circle to any point on the circle. The distance from the center to that point is called the *radius*.

The distance around a circle is called the *circumference*. The word circumference comes from the Latin word circum, meaning "around". A circle contains 360 degrees. A *semicircle* is half a circle, so it contains 180 degrees. The *diameter* is a line that starts from any point on a circle, goes through the center, and ends on the exact opposite side of the circle. So a diameter equals two radii. When two or more diameters are drawn from different points on a circle, they form angles. When you slice a round pizza, you usually slice along several diameters. If you slice a pizza into eight equal pieces, each piece will have a 45-degree angle.

We can use circles to measure other things. Each time your bicycle wheel rolls around once, you know how far you have traveled if you know the wheel's circumference. The same principle is used in

---

半径。

　　绕圆一周的距离叫做周长。单词"周长"来源于拉丁语"圆周"，意思是"周围"。一个圆周有360°。半圆就半个圆周，所以它是180°。直径是从圆上任意一点开始，穿过圆心，到达圆周上正对面一点的距离。所以直径等于半径的二倍。当在一个圆周上从不同起点画两条或两条以上的直径时，它们之间就形成了夹角。当你去切一个圆形的披萨时，你通常会沿着多条直径去切。如果你将一个披萨切成8等份，每块披萨都有一个45°的角。

　　我们能用圆来测量其他的东西。如果你知道车轮的周长，每当你的自行车轮转动一圈，你就能算出你已经行驶了多远。汽车的里程计数器使用

---

radius *n.* 半径（长度）　　　　　　　circumference *n.* 圆周；圆周长
semicircle *n.* 半圆；半圆形　　　　　　diameter *n.* 直径；对径

the mileage *counter* of a car.

A *compass* is an instrument used for drawing circles. This compass is different from the compass that shows direction. It has two legs connected by a *pivot*. One leg has a pointed end that holds the compass in place on a piece of paper, and the other leg holds a pencil. As you turn the compass, the pencil will trace a circle.

The distance around a circle is about three times the length of the diameter. This is true for all circles. If you divide the circumference by the diameter, you will get a number that is approximately 3.14. This is the value that is often used for the number known as pi, or p. The full value for pi cannot be written down, since it goes on forever to the right of the *decimal point*. Pi is always the same number, no matter how large the circle.

的是相同的原理。

　　圆规是一种用来画圆的工具。这与指示方向的罗盘是有区别的。它是由一个支点连接两条腿而形成的。其中一条腿的末端是尖的，它能够把圆规固定在一张纸上。另一条腿上装有一支铅笔。当你转动圆规时，铅笔将画出一个圆。

　　一个圆的周长大约是直径的三倍。这条规则对所有的圆都是成立的。如果你用周长除以直径，你将得到一个约等于3.14的数。这个值常被一个叫做π的数字使用。π的真值无法完全写出，因为它的小数点右边的数字是无限不循环的，永远不会终止。无论圆有多大，π值都是不变的。

---

counter *n.* （电子）计数器；计算器
pivot *n.* 支点；枢轴

compass *n.* 圆规；罗盘
decimal point 小数点

26

Let's Have Some Wheel Fun

For thousands of years, people have used the wheel as an *aid* for moving themselves or other objects. Wheels are used for work and for *recreation*. An example of a fun wheel is the Ferris wheel. This *amusement park* ride is basically a large circle with passenger seats attached to it. People riding in the seats travel the entire

让我们一起玩摩天轮吧

几千年来，人们用轮子作为辅助来移动他们自己或者是其他物体。轮子被用在工作和娱乐中。摩天轮就是一个娱乐轮子的例子。游乐园里的过山车主体就是一个固定有很多乘客坐椅的大圆环。随着轮子一圈一圈转动，乘客坐在坐椅上也经过了轮子的整个圆周。

---

aid *n.* 助手；辅助设备   recreation *n.* 娱乐；消遣
amusement park 游乐场；娱乐园

circumference of the wheel as it turns around and around.

The Ferris wheel was introduced at the World's Fair of 1893, in Chicago, Illinois. It was built by George Ferris, who got the idea from looking at merry-go-rounds. Ferris believed that a *vertical* wheel could be as much fun as a *horizontal* wheel, if not more fun.

The diameter of the original Ferris wheel was 250 feet—making it the largest wheel in the world at the time. The circumference was 785 feet. Thirty-six wooden cars held about 60 riders each. More than 2,000 people could ride the wheel at one time.

Ferris wheels are divided by many *spokes*, as on a bicycle. The spokes running across the wheel through the center form many *angles*. The number of angles depends on the number of spokes on the wheel.

摩天轮是在1893年伊利诺斯州的芝加哥举办的世界博览会中被引进的。它是由乔治·法利士建造的，法利士是在观察旋转木马时得到的灵感。法利士认为一个竖直放置的轮子即使不能带来比水平轮子更多的乐趣，至少能带来和水平轮子一样的乐趣。

原始的法利士摩天轮的直径是250英尺，这也使它成为当时世界上最大的轮子。这个轮子的周长是785英尺。轮子上固定有36辆木质小车，每辆能装载60名乘客。这个摩天轮一次能装载超过2 000名乘客。

法利士摩天轮上有很多将圆分割的轮辐，就像自行车轮上的轮辐一样。横跨轮子并穿过轮中心的 轮辐形成了很多角。角的个数取决于轮子上的轮辐数。

---

vertical *adj.* 竖的；直立的
spoke *n.* 轮辐；辐条

horizontal *adj.* 水平的；横的
angle *n.* 角；斜角

27

Distances and Light-Years in Space

Astronomy is the science of *outer space*. *Astronomers* are people who study the universe—the solar system, the stars, the planets. They try to understand how large the universe is and how many years it has existed. Astronomers don't measure distance in outer space the way we measure distance on Earth. Have you

太空中的距离和光年

天文学是关于宇宙空间的科学。天文学家就是那些研究宇宙——太阳系、恒星、行星的那些人。他们试图了解宇宙究竟有多大，已经存在了多少年。天文学家并不采用我们衡量地球上距离的方式来衡量外太空的距离。你曾经听到过某人说某些东西是"天文数字"吗？如

---

outer space 外层空间；太空   astronomer *n.* 天文学家

ever heard someone say something is "*astronomical*"? If you want to say that something is really big, such as distances in space, you can use the word astronomical.

Our sun is a star. It is closer to Earth than any other star in the universe. The sun is about 93 million miles away. The next nearest star after the sun is about 24 *trillion* miles away! Light from the sun has to travel pretty far to reach Earth. Light travels quickly, though— about 186,282 miles per second. The speed of light is always the same.

Scientists use the *term light-years* to refer to how far light travels in an Earth year. Astronomers use light-years as a way to measure the huge distances in outer space.

果你想说明某样东西非常大，例如太空，你就可以使用天文数字这个词。

我们的太阳是一颗恒星，相对于宇宙中所有其他恒星来说，它离地球是最近的，太阳距离地球约9 300万英里。在太阳之后离地球最近的恒星离地球24兆英里。太阳光需要历经相当远的路程才能到达地球表面，尽管光传播得很快，约186 282英里/秒。光的速度是一个固定不变的常量。

科学家用光年来代表地球上一年时间里光传播的距离。天文学家把光年作为测量宇宙中遥远距离的方法。

---

astronomical *adj.* （数量、价格等）极其巨大的
term *n.* 词语；术语

trillion *n.* 万亿；兆
light-year *n.* 光年

To find how many *actual* miles a light-year is, first calculate the number of seconds in a year: 60 seconds × 60 minutes × 24 hours × 365.25 days in a year = 31,557,600 seconds. Then multiply the number of seconds in a year by the speed of light (186,282 miles per second). So, one light-year is about 5,878,612,843,200 miles. That means in one year, light can travel about 6 trillion miles through space. But this is still only about one-fourth the distance to the nearest star to our sun. When talking about the size of the universe, a single light-year is very small.

Many astronomers believe that the universe began with an *explosive blast*, known as the Big Bang. The Big Bang, they believe, created all the matter that would become planets and stars. Astronomers think

---

　　为了弄清1光年的实际距离到底有多少英里，首先要计算一年中有多少秒：60秒×60分钟×24小时×365.25天=31 557 600秒。接下来拿一年中的秒数值乘以光速（186 282英里/秒）。因此，1光年大约是5 878 612 843 200英里。这表示在一年里，光能在宇宙中传播大约6兆英里的距离。但这仅仅是距离地球最近的恒星太阳与地球之间距离的1/4。当谈论宇宙的大小这类话题时，1光年就显得非常小了。

　　很多天文学家认为宇宙起源于一场特大爆炸，也被称作创世大爆炸。他们认为这场大爆炸产生的所有物质后来都变成了行星和恒星。天文学家

---

actual *adj.* 实际的；真实的　　　　　explosive *adj.* 爆炸性的；易爆炸的
blast *n.* 爆炸

the universe is now about 11.2 billion years old. Light that is reaching us from the farthest known *galaxies* has been traveling for more than 20 billion years.

A galaxy is a collection of billions of stars and clouds of gases and dust. The Milky Way is the name of our galaxy. It includes our sun, with its nine known planets, and billions of other stars. Look at the stars some night. Some of the light you see may have started out from stars billions of years ago.

认为宇宙已存在了约112亿年。到达地球上的来自已知最远星系的光已经传播了超过200亿年。

一个星系是由数十亿恒星、气体云和尘埃共同构成的。我们所在的星系叫做银河系。它包含了太阳和它的9颗已知行星，还有其他数十亿恒星。有时候在夜晚看星星，你看到的一些光亮可能在数十亿年前就已经发出了。

galaxy *n.* 星系

28

Finding the Mean Distance From the Sun

There are nine known *planets* in our solar system. We *generally* think of them in order by their distance from the sun. All the planets orbit the sun in the same direction. Also, each is closer to the sun at some times than at other times. This is why scientists talk about a planet's mean distance from the sun. The mean is the

寻找和太阳之间的平均距离

在我们生存的太阳系中有九大已知的行星。我们通常根据它们与太阳之间的距离大小来考虑它们。所有行星都沿同一方向绕太阳旋转。而且，每个行星与太阳的距离在某些时段会更近些，其余时间又会远些。这就是为什么科学家讨论一个行星和太阳之间的平均距离。平均值就是两个或两个以上数字的平均数。在恒星的轨道这个情境中，平均值

---

planet *n.* 行星

generally *adv.* 通常；普遍地

average of two or more numbers. In the case of a planet's *orbit*, the mean is the average of the greatest distance and the shortest distance from the planet to the sun.

Earth's mean distance from the sun is 93 million miles. But astronomers do not like to use such big numbers when talking about the *immense* distances in space. That is why they measure these distances in smaller astronomical units. One astronomical unit, or 1AU, is Earth's mean distance from the sun. In other words, 1AU = 93 million miles.

When Earth is closest to the sun, the distance between the two is about 91.3 million miles. At the point in its orbit farthest from the sun, Earth is 94.5 million miles away. Scientists take an average of these numbers, (91.3 + 94.5) ÷ 2, and then round the *quotient* to 93 million miles.

就是行星和太阳之间的最大距离和最小距离的平均数。

地球与太阳之间的平均距离是9 300万英里。但当谈论空间中的特大距离时，天文学家不喜欢使用如此巨大的数字。这就是他们使用更小的天文单位来衡量距离的原因。一个天文单位，或者说是1AU，就是地球与太阳之间的平均距离。换句话说，1AU=93 000 000英里。

当地球距离太阳最近时，二者之间的距离大约是91 300 000英里。在环绕轨道上距离太阳最远的那一点，地球与太阳之间的距离是94 500 000英里。科学家们取这些数字的平均数，(91.3+94.5)÷2，然后将得到的商四舍五入，结果是93 000 000英里。

---

orbit *n.* （天体等运行的）轨道　　　　immense *adj.* 极大的；巨大的
quotient *n.* 商（除法所得的结果）

29

What Do Business Accountants Do?

Accountants *gather* and *organize* *financial* information for company owners. This information helps owners understand the finances of their company. In a way, an accountant records the history of a company in dollar amounts collected and paid out.

会计师是做什么的呢？

会计师为公司的老板收集并整理财务信息。这类信息能够帮助老板掌握公司的财务状况。总的来说，会计师以美元记录公司的每一笔收入和支出。

---

accountant *n.* 会计；会计师　　　　gather *v.* 收集；归拢
organize *v.* 组织；整理　　　　financial *adj.* 财务的；金融的

Business accountants list all the money a company has made or lost on a form called a general *ledger*. This form shows *asset* accounts and *liability* accounts. Assets may be money that is gained or materials that are worth money. Liability is money owed to some person or another company.

Some costs appear on both the assets side and the liabilities side of the ledger. Others show up on only one side. Buying a machine for $100 in cash would show up on only the assets side. The machine's value—$100—would be added to the company's equipment assets. The same amount would be subtracted from its *cash* assets. The net change in total assets would be zero. However, if the company bought the machine on credit, both sides of the ledger would be affected. The equipment assets would increase by $100, but the liabilities would also increase by $100.

会计师以总账的形式罗列一个公司所有的盈利和亏损。这个表格显示了资产账户和负债账户。资产是公司赚得的钱或是公司里值钱的材料。负债就是欠别人或其他公司的钱。

有一些花费在总账的资产类别和负债类别中同时出现。其他的花费则只在一类中出现。购买一台机器使用的100美元现金只会在资产类别中出现。机器的价值——100美元，会加到公司的设备资产中。与此同时，相同的数额会从现金资产中扣除。总资产的净变化量将会是0。然而，如果公司是通过贷款的方式购买机器的，总账中的两类资产都会受影响。设备资产会增加100美元，但同时负债也会增加100美元。

---

ledger *n.* 收支总账；分类账簿

liability *n.* 负债；债务

asset *n.* 资产；财产

cash *n.* 现金；资金

An accountant records every change that involves money as both a *debit* item and a credit item. These debits and credits are called *"entries"* because they are entered into the general ledger. A credit entry may be money available to spend. A debit entry shows how money was spent. This system of accounting is known as double-entry accounting.

Keeping financial records is the most common task of accountants. However, many accountants work in specific areas. Some large companies hire accountants to design record-keeping computer programs for them. Many accountants work on creating better budgets for companies. Others may focus on ways to increase a company's *profits*. Tax accountants prepare tax returns. They may advise company *presidents* about how new business *deals* may affect taxes. Tax accountants must know a lot about laws that apply to

---

会计记录包括借方项目和贷方项目的涉及钱的每一笔交易。这些借款和贷款被称为"分录",因为它们都进了总账。贷方分录可能是能够使用的钱,借方分录显示的是已经花费了的钱。这个结算体系也被称为双录结算。

做财务记录是会计师们最常见的任务。然而,许多会计师是在特定领域工作的。一些大型公司雇用会计师为他们开发计算机记账程序。很多会计师致力于为公司创造更好的预算。还有一些可能致力于提高公司的利润。税务会计师筹备纳税申报表,他们会给公司的董事长一些关于新的交易将会如何影响税款的建议。税务会计师必须了解适用于税务的诸多法律

---

debit *n.* 借记;借项　　　　　　　　　　　entry *n.* 账目;记录
profit *n.* 利润;赢利

taxes.

Some accountants work as *auditors*. These people study financial *statements* to make sure they are complete and correct. Auditors who work in a company make sure that the company's accounting plan is being followed. Outside auditors make sure a company's financial statements are correct and that the company follows the accepted accounting rules. Accountants have a lot of responsibility, so they must be well trained. They must pass a difficult test before they can get a license.

条款。

　　有些会计师从事审计工作。这些人审核财务报表以确保它们的完整性和正确性。公司内部的审计人员能够保证公司的会计计划是能够具体实施的。外部的审计人员确保公司财务报表的正确性，并且确保公司遵循国家认可的会计规则。会计师要承担很多责任，因此他们必须受到良好的培训。在得到许可证之前他们必须通过一场难度很大的考试。

---

president *n.* 董事长；总裁　　　　　　deal *n.* 交易；协议

auditor *n.* 审计员；稽核员　　　　　statement *n.* 报表；清单

30

Home Office Deductions

Working from a home office can have tax *rewards*. A person with a home office could *deduct* some of the costs of the home office from his or her taxes.

The Internal Revenue Service has rules about what counts as a home office. The worker must use the office for business only. Tax rules allow a worker to deduct a

家庭办公减免

在家庭办公室办公的人能获得一些税务回报。一个拥有家庭办公室的人可以从他或她的税款中免去部分有关家庭办公室的花费。

国内税务服务中有如何界定家庭办公室的相关规则。这间家庭办公室只能被工作者用来办公。根据办公区域在整个房屋中所占的百分比，税务

---

reward *n.* 回报；报酬   deduct *v.* 扣除；减去

percentage of certain costs for the home according to the percentage of the house that is used as office space. Imagine that a person's house has 2,000 square feet. The office fills 200 square feet. To find the percentage of tax *deduction*, divide the total square feet of the house by the square feet of the office (2,000 ÷ 200 = 10). This means that 10 percent of the costs for the home can be deducted from the taxes.

The worker can also deduct 10 percent of the direct costs of the home office. For example, let's say that one year office machines ($11,000), *heat* and electricity ($3,590), and a new *carpet* ($1,720) for the home office came to $16,310. The worker would be allowed to subtract 10 percent of this amount, or $1,631, from the taxes.

法则允许工作者减免一定百分比的家庭花费。假设一个人的房屋是2 000平方英尺，其中办公室占地200平方英尺。为计算税款减免百分比，用房屋的总平方英尺数除以办公室的平方英尺数（2 000÷200=10）。这意味着家庭花费的10%可以从税款中免除。

工作者也能减免办公室直接花费的10%。例如，我们假设一年中，办公室机器费用是11 000美元，供暖和电费一共是3 590美元，为办公室添置的新地毯是1 720美元，这些加在一起就是16 310美元。工作者将被允许从税收中免去这部分花费的10%，即1 631美元。

---

percentage *n.* 百分率；百分比   deduction *n.* 扣除（额）；减去（数）
heat *n.* 供暖；供暖系统   carpet *n.* 地毯

31

Comparing Professional Athletes' Pay: Men Versus Women

In the U.S. *workforce*, women earn 77 cents for each dollar a man earns doing the same job. In professional sports that *gap* is even wider. Let's take a look at the mathematics behind the *current figures* for earnings in individual and team sports.

There are no women on the Forbes Magazine's 2004 list of the World's 50 Best

男女职业运动员的收入对比

美国劳动人口中，同样的工作，女性员工只挣到男性员工薪水的77%。这一差距在职业运动中更大。让我们来看一下，目前个人运动与团体运动中收入数字的数学运算。

2004年福布斯杂志公布的高薪运动员排行榜中，前五十名内没有女运动员。高尔夫运动员泰格·伍兹以年薪8 000万美元高居榜首。相比之

---

workforce *n.* 劳动力；劳动人口
current *adj.* 现时的；目前的

gap *n.* 差距；距离
figure *n.* 数字；数目

Paid Athletes. The top-paid *athlete* is *golfer* Tiger Woods at $80 million a year. By *contrast*, the highest-paid woman golfer, Annika Sorenstam, made $5 million. That's about 6 percent of Woods's *earnings*. The top-paid woman in sports is tennis player Serena Williams at $9.5 million. Williams's earnings were just 12 percent of Woods's. The top-paid tennis player, Andre Agassi, made $28 million. So Williams made about 34 percent of Agassi's earnings.

What about the prize money for top golf and tennis players? The average total prize money for a recent five-year period in tennis was $63,031,000 for men and $41,000,000 for women. That puts women tennis players' pay at about 65 percent of men's. The average total prize money for the same five-year period in golf was $108,572,200

下，薪酬最高的女高尔夫选手安妮卡·索伦斯坦的年薪也只有500万美元，约为伍兹收入的6%。收入最高的女运动员是网球选手塞雷娜·威廉姆斯，她的年薪为950万美元，仅是伍兹的12%。薪酬最高的男网球选手安德烈·阿加西的年收入为2 800万美元，也就是说，威廉姆斯的收入大约只是阿加西收入的34%。

顶级高尔夫球运动员和网球运动员的奖金情况如何？男网球运动员近五年的平均奖金总额为63 031 000美元；而女运动员的则为41 000 000美元，大约是男运动员奖金额的65%。在同样的五年里，男高尔夫球运动员的平均总奖金总额为108 572 200美元，而女性运动员的为32 817 400

athlete *n.* 运动员   golfer *n.* 高尔夫球员

contrast *n.* 对比；对照   earnings *n.* 收入；薪金

for men and $32,817,400 for women. That puts women golfers' pay at only about 30 percent of men's. Still, it's not as bad as the gap between Sorenstam and Woods.

Women's and men's *professional* team sports show an even bigger pay gap. *For instance*, in 2003 the Women's National Basketball Association (WNBA) paid its players an average *salary* of $46,000 for the season. The men's NBA paid its players an average of $4.5 million. Women players' pay was about 1 percent of men players' pay.

Why is the pay gap in professional sports so large? The main reason is the market. Unlike jobs where men and women are making the same product or doing the same service, in professional sports

---

美元，大约仅为男运动员奖金额的30%。尽管如此，这也不如索伦斯坦和伍兹之间的收入差距大。

男女职业团体运动的收入差距更大。如2003年美国女子职业篮球联赛给运动员的平均薪金为每赛季46 000美元。而美国男子职业篮球联赛给运动员的平均薪金为每个赛季4 500 000美元。女运动员的薪金约为男运动员的1%。

为什么职业运动收入差距会这么大？主要原因是市场需求。与男女员工同样生产同一产品或提供同一服务的工作不同，职业运动中运动员本身就是产品。不论公平与否，运动员的薪金是由该运动的观众和收视率决定

---

professional *adj.* 职业的　　　　　　　　　for instance 例如；比如
salary *n.* 薪水；薪金

the players themselves are the product. *Fair* or not, the money that the players make is based on *crowds* and TV *ratings*. Until women's sports draw as many fans as men's sports draw, women will make less money.

The good news for women athletes is that women's sports are becoming more popular. The WNBA has been around only since 1997 and is still finding its market. It has less than half the teams and games of the NBA. As the sport grows, its players will likely get paid more money.

的。在女子运动能吸引与男子运动同样多的观众之前，女运动员的薪金也会相对较少。

值得女运动员高兴的是女子运动正日渐兴盛。女子职业篮球联赛1997年才兴起，并一直在开拓市场。其球队数目和比赛场次不及男子篮球联赛的一半。随着这项运动的发展，女运动员的收入会更高。

---

fair *adj.* 公正的；公平的
rating *n.* 收视率；收听率

crowd *n.* 群众；观众

32

Keeping Score in Golf

If you don't know how to add *negative* numbers, you might not have much fun playing golf. A *round* of golf is usually made up of 18 holes, and golfers complete one hole at a time. The score for a round is the total *strokes*, or *swings* of the golf club, that a golfer makes—from the opening tee shot on the first hole to the final putt on the

高尔夫计分

如果不知道如何加负数，你可能就不会对打高尔夫球有那么多兴趣。一轮球赛通常有18个洞，选手每次完成一洞。一轮的得分是指总击球数或挥杆次数，即高尔夫球手从第一洞的开球到第18洞的推球

---

negative *adj.* 负数的；负的
stroke *n.* 击球

round *n.* （高尔夫球赛的）一场
swing *n.* 挥动；挥击

18th.

Each hole on a golf *course* is *assigned* a number called par. Par is the number of strokes that a *capable* golfer would need on average to finish the hole. An excellent score is under par—that is, fewer strokes than par.

Scoring in golf is *cumulative*. Let's say you are playing on a course where the first hole is par 4. If you sink the ball in two strokes, your score is -2, because you finished at two under par. The second hole is par 5. You finish that hole in ten strokes! So your score for this hole is +5. Your cumulative score is +3, because (-2) + (+5) = +3. The third hole is par 3, and you need only one stroke—a hole in one! Add -2 to your score. Your cumulative score is +1 as you proceed to the fourth hole.

入洞的过程中获得的总分。

高尔夫球场上每洞都编有一个号码，称之为规定击球次数。规定击球次数是指有能力的高尔夫选手完成每洞所需的平均击球次数。高分是指低于标准杆数，即击球次数少于规定击球次数。

高尔夫比赛计分采用累积法。举个例子，你进行高尔夫球比赛时，第一洞的标准杆数为4。如果你两杆进洞，就得到-2分，因为你完成一洞的击球次数比标准杆少两次。第二洞的标准杆数为5次，你若10杆进洞，就得到+5分。因为(-2)+(+5)=+3，所以你的累计分数为+3分。第三洞的标准杆数为3，而你只需一杆进洞。在之前的分数上加上-2分，那么进行第四洞前的累计分数就为+1分。

---

course *n.* 高尔夫球场　　　　　assign *v.* 分配；指定
capable *adj.* 有能力的；能胜任的　　cumulative *adj.* 累积的；渐增的

33

DeShawn's Paycheck

After graduating from college, DeShawn recently started his first regular full-time job. DeShawn's *annual* salary is \$36,036, so his weekly earnings before *deductions*, or *gross* pay, equals \$693 (\$36,036 ÷ 52 = \$693). When he received his first *paycheck*, he was not surprised to find his net pay was a lot less than

德沙恩的工资

大学毕业后，德沙恩开始了他第一份全职工作。他年薪或税前总收入为36 036美元，所以，他税前每周的收入为693美元（36036美元÷52 = 693 美元）。收到第一份工资时，他并未对自己的实际收入远低于693美元感到惊讶。他看了随工资寄来的工资明细，找到了

---

annual *adj.* 每年的；年度的 deduction *n.* 扣除（额）；减去（数）
gross *adj.* 总的；全部的 paycheck *n.* 工资；收入

$693. He looked at the check *record* that came with the paycheck and found several deductions listed. These are amounts that were *subtracted* from DeShawn's gross pay.

The first deduction on the check was for FICA (Federal Insurance Contributions Act). This deduction is for Social Security, which pays money to retired people. The FICA tax rate on DeShawn's earnings is 7.65 percent. So $53.01 in FICA tax was deducted from DeShawn's paycheck.

Both *federal* and state income taxes were also subtracted from DeShawn's gross pay. Federal income tax is paid to the U.S. government to support its work and to fund various national programs. The amount is *calculated* from tax tables that are based on a person's yearly earnings. DeShawn will pay $3,884 in federal income taxes a year. That amount, divided by the number of weeks

---

扣款项目列表。这些就是从德沙恩总收入中扣除的金额。

工资明细上第一项扣款是联邦社会保障捐款法规定的税款。这一款项是为退休人员提供的社保款。联邦社会保障税是德沙恩工资的7.65%，因此要从他的工资中扣除53.01美元的联邦社会保障税。

德沙恩的总收入还要扣除联邦和州政府的个人所得税。联邦个人所得税用以支付政府开支，并为各种国家项目提供资金。纳税金额的计算是依个人年收入而定的，德沙恩每年要向联邦政府上缴税款3 884美元。年税额除以一年总周数，即为每周纳税74.69美元（3 884美元÷52=74.69美元）。州政府个人所得税则用于管理州政府项目。这一税款也是按年收入

---

record *n.* 记录；记载　　　　　　subtract *v.* 减；减去
federal *adj.* 联邦制的；联邦政府的　　calculate *v.* 计算；算出

in a year, comes to $74.69 a week ($3,884 ÷ 52 = $74.69). State income taxes are used to help run state government programs. They are also based on yearly gross income, but the percentage deducted is smaller than for the federal income tax. DeShawn's state income tax deduction is $38.19 a week.

The company DeShawn works for pays for basic health *insurance* for all workers. This insurance covers major *medical* costs for workers. People who work for the company can choose to increase the amount of insurance they agree to pay. When he was hired, DeShawn chose extra medical and *dental* insurance. He pays $1,404 a year for the additional health insurance, or $27 a week.

DeShawn noted that the last deduction is for his *savings* plan. This plan lets DeShawn send part of his earnings directly to a savings account at his bank. DeShawn believes he will save more easily if

---

计算，但其扣税的比率低于联邦政府。德沙恩每周要向州政府上缴税款38.19美元。

德沙恩所在的公司为全体员工支付基本健康保险。这种保险涵盖了员工主要的医疗费用。员工可以按自己的意愿选择增加保险额。一入职，德沙恩就选择了额外医疗和牙科保险。他每年支付额外健康保险费1 404美元，也就是每周27美元。

德沙恩注意到最后一项扣款是用于支付他的存款计划。这一计划让德沙恩把收入的一部分直接存入了他的银行存款账户。德沙恩认为从工资直接扣款更有利于他的存款计划。他每周都有50美元直接存入账户，一年下

---

insurance *n.* 保险；保险金
dental *adj.* 牙齿的；牙科的

medical *adj.* 医学的；医疗的
savings *n.* 积蓄；存款

101

the money is deducted *straight* from his paycheck. He has $50 a week *deposited* directly into his savings *account*. His savings will total $2,600 each year ($50 × 52 = $2,600).

The deductions from DeShawn's paycheck total $242.89. DeShawn divided the total deductions by the gross pay, $693, and found that his weekly deductions equal about 35 percent of his gross pay.

来就有2 600美元的存款（50美元×52=2600美元）。

　　从德沙恩工资中扣除的总额为242.89美元。他用总扣除额除以总收入693美元得到每周的扣除额约为总收入的35%。

---

straight *adv.* 直接地　　　　　　deposit *v.* 存储；将（钱）存入银行
account *n.* 账户；户头

34

Tracking Your Checking Account Balance

When buying *items* on-line, people today have the *option* of paying with a credit card, with a *debit* card, or with a personal check. Regardless of what method is used, a person buying an item must have a bank account and *sufficient* money in the account. This example will follow Maria, who likes paying with checks.

跟踪账户余额

如今人们网购时可以选择使用信用卡，借记卡或支票来支付。无论采取哪种方式，购物时都要有银行账户，而且账户里要存有足够的金额。玛利亚就是这样的例子，她喜欢用支票付款。她将钱存入活期存款账户，这样当她签支票时银行会从她账户里扣除这部分钱并转入到支票支付的个人或公司。玛利亚从支票簿的记录中减去金额。存钱时她再

---

item *n.* 一件商品（或物品）　　　　option *n.* 选择；取舍

debit *n.* 借记；借方　　　　　　　　sufficient *adj.* 足够的；充足的

Maria deposits money into her *checking account*. When she writes a check, the bank deducts the amount of the check from Maria's account and pays the money to the person or company to whom she wrote the check. Maria deducts the amount of the check from the record in her *checkbook*. When she deposits money, she adds that amount to the account. By using simple math, Maria keeps track of her bank balance.

Maria opened her checking account in June with $450.23. During July she deposited $1,200, so her new balance was $1,650.23 ($450.23 + $1,200). Then she wrote 15 checks totaling $1,084.37. After writing each check, she calculated her new balance by deducting the amount of that check from the previous balance. After all of the checks were deducted, she had a balance of $565.86. The bank sends Maria a statement each month that shows every deposit or *withdrawal* made in the checking account.

将金额加到账户上。通过简单的数学运算，她就可以跟踪到银行账户的收支平衡。

玛利亚6月份开户时账户余额为450.23美元。她7月份存入了1 200美元，所以新的余额应为1 650.23美元（450.23美元+1 200美元）。之后她签了总额为1 084.37美元的15张支票。每写下一张支票，她就会计算出从账户中扣除金额后的余额。扣除所有支票金额后，她的余额为565.86美元。银行每月都会给她寄账单，账单记录了她账户上每笔存款与支出。

---

checking account 活期存款账户   checkbook *n.* 支票簿
withdrawal *n.* 提款；取款

35

The Money Behind the Movies

A Hollywood *studio* may spend $250 million or more to make a film, or it may spend as little as $200,000. The first is considered a high-budget film, and the second a low-budget film. A studio makes a *budget* for every film, trying to *judge* how much it will cost.

In film budgets, there are two types of

电影的幕后花费

好莱坞的制片厂制作一部电影可能花费2.5亿美元甚至更多，也可能仅花20万美元。前者称为高成本电影，后者则为低成本电影。制片厂会为每部电影做预算，力求估算出每部电影的成本。

电影预算主要分为两类。其中最主要的开支为作家、导演、制片人以

---

studio *n.* 制片厂；摄影棚

judge *v.* 估计；估价

budget *n.* 预算

costs. Costs such as the salaries for writers, directors, *producers*, and top actors appear in the top part of the budget. These are called above-the-line costs. The *crew*, supplies, advertising, and other costs related to the film appear in the lower part of the budget. These are known as below-the-line costs.

Different kinds of films need different kinds of budgets, because *expenses* vary for each type of film. The budget for a cartoon movie would include salaries for actors to do the voices of characters and for artists to draw the characters. An action film with special *effects* usually costs more than a romantic comedy. Studios have to figure out what they will spend in each category of the budget. For example, studios often spend $50 million or more to advertise a movie. The advertising budget for *The Lord of the Rings: Return of the*

及大牌演员的薪酬，我们称其为常规开支。预算中所占预算比重较少的开支为工作人员薪酬、道具、广告等，我们称其为幕后花费。

由于经费随电影类别的变化而变化，所以电影的类型不同，预算也不尽相同。一部卡通电影的预算包括配音演员、动画制作人员的酬劳。一部有特效的动作电影的开支要高于一部浪漫喜剧片。制片厂必须在预算中清楚地知道每笔花销。例如，他们常常花费5 000万美元甚至更多来宣传一部电影。《指环王——王者归来》仅在美国的广告预算就高达7 500万美

producer *n.* 制片人；监制人
expense *n.* 支出；花费

crew *n.* 一组工作人员
effect *n.* 效果

King was $75 million in the United States alone.

Budgets provide studios with a good understanding of exactly what they are spending on a film minute by minute. If the film has a production budget of $15 million and runs 100 minutes, that would mean each minute of the film costs $150,000 to make ($15,000,000 ÷ 100 = $150,000). Studios spend a lot of money, but they also hope to earn a profit.

To *figure out* how successful a movie is, studios look at the film's profit *ratio*. This compares the movie's gross profit to its budget. A movie's gross profit is the amount it earns in ticket *sales*. The studio's goal is to keep the film's *costs* down and the ticket sales up. Profit ratio is calculated by dividing the film's gross profit by its production cost. For example, a film grossing $420 million, with a production

---

元。

　　预算为制片厂详细地列出了制作电影每一分钟所需的花费。若电影的制作预算为1 500万美元，片长100分钟，那么每分钟就要花费15万美元（1 500万美元÷100=15万美元）。虽然制片厂花了大笔资金，但是他们也希望获得利润。

　　制片厂依据电影的利润率来判断电影的成功与否。利润率是电影总收益和其预算额的比值。这里电影的总收益指的是其票房收入。制片厂的目

---

figure out　估计；弄明白　　　　　　　　　ratio　*n.* 比；比率
sales　*n.* 销售量　　　　　　　　　　　　cost　*n.* 成本；价格

budget of $50 million, has a profit ratio of 8.4 (420 ÷ 50 = 8.4). *The Titanic grossed* $600 million. It cost $200 million to make. That's a profit ratio of 3 (600 ÷ 200 = 3). Since 1990, only 15 movies with total ticket sales of at least $20 million have had profit ratios higher than 10.

标是降低电影成本，提高票房。电影的总收益除以它的制作成本得出利润率。例如，一部电影的总利润为4.2亿美元，制作成本为5 000万美元，那么它的利润率为8.4（420÷50=8.4）。《泰坦尼克号》的总利润为6亿美元，制作成本为2亿美元，那么其利润率为3（600÷200=3）。1990年以来，仅有15部电影的票房超过2 000万美元，且利润率高于10。

---

grossed　*v.* 总共赚得

36

Making a Household Budget

A budget is a way to set *financial* goals and to keep track of where money goes. Most *household* budgets are made with columns related to categories such as money paid out for rent, food, and phone.

Mike works at a *record* store and earns $400 per week. His *net* salary, after taxes, is

家庭预算的制订

预算是一种制订财务目标并跟踪资金去向的方式。有些家庭预算，诸如房租、食物开销及电话费等往往会分类列出。

麦克在一家唱片店工作，每周工资为400美元，他的税后净收入为每月1 350美元。每月公寓房租用掉500美元。房租是固定支出，因为每月

---

financial *adj.* 财务的；财政的   household *n.* 家庭

record *n.* 唱片   net *adj.* （尤指金钱）纯的；净的

$1,350 per month. He *rents* an apartment for $500 a month. Rent is called a *fixed* expense because it is the same amount every month. After paying rent, Mike has $850 for his other expenses—food, phone, electricity, clothes, entertainment, and savings. These are called *variable* expenses. They change from month to month.

To create his budget, Mike began by writing down all his expenses. This helped him figure out the different categories of his budget. Then Mike decided how much to spend on each category. Each month Mike writes down what he spends and compares it to what he budgeted. This month, Mike was under budget on food, but his electric bill was high. His budget allowed for him to spend $1,200, but his actual expenses totaled $1,272. He had a $72 *deficit*. He spent more than he had budgeted. Next month Mike plans to follow his budget more carefully.

都支付同样多的钱。扣除房租后，食物、电话费、电费、服装费、娱乐和存款等费用还需花费850美元。这部分费用为弹性支出，因为每月支出会有变化。

为了制订预算，麦克将全部开销都写下来。这样可以帮助他将预算进行分类。由此他就可以决定每项的费用。麦克每月都会把实际开支记下来，和预算作比较。这个月，麦克的食物开销低于预算，电费却很高。预算开支为1 200美元，但实际消费却是1 272美元。他有72美元的赤字，即他的花销超过了预算，麦克打算下个月更谨慎地执行预算。

---

rent *v.* 租用；出租
variable *adj.* 可变的；可更改的

fixed *adj.* 固定的；不变的
deficit *n.* 赤字；缺乏

37

The Electoral College

Here is a common situation. A teacher gives two choices for a *field trip*. In this case, the choices are to go to the science museum or to visit a nearby university. The teacher leaves the decision to the class, and the students *vote*. There are 31 students. Eighteen students, a little more than half, vote for the field trip to the

---

选举团

一种常见的情况是，老师会在安排实地考察时给学生提供两种选择。比如，可选择去科学博物馆或者去参观附近的大学。老师让学生自己投票选择。全班有31名学生，有略超半数的18名学生投票去

---

field trip 野外考察；户外教学   vote *v.* 投票；投票决定

science museum. The choice with the most votes is the winner.

In the 2000 presidential *election*, Al Gore received 50,999,897 votes, and George W. Bush received 50,456,002 votes. Gore received 543,895 more votes than Bush did. Yet, George W. Bush became president. Why? In the United States, the president is not elected on the basis of total votes. Presidents are selected by the *electoral college*. The word college is from a Latin word meaning "society".

The people who wrote the U.S. *Constitution* created the electoral college in 1787. This measure gave each state a certain number of electoral votes on the basis of two factors. Each state was given one vote for each *senator*. This gave each state two votes, since there are two U.S. senators from each state. The other electoral votes

---

参观科学博物馆。票数较多的一方胜出。

2000年总统大选的时候，阿尔·戈登获得50 999 897票，乔治·W·布什获得50 456 002票。戈登比布什高出543 895票，但布什却成了总统。这是为什么？因为在美国，总统选举并不是靠总票数而是由选举团来决定的。"选举团（college）"这个词源于拉丁语，意为团队。

选举团于1787年由《美国宪法》的制定者建立。这一办法依据两个因素分配给每个州一定数目的选票。各州仅有两名参议员名额，而且各州的参议员每人仅一张选票。这样每州有两张选票。另一类选票分配给各州

---

election *n.* 选举；选举活动
constitution *n.* 宪法；章程

electoral college 选举团
senator *n.* 参议员

come from the number of U.S. *representatives* each state has. The state's population determines this number. So the greater a state's population, the more *electoral* votes it gets.

California, for example, has 55 electoral votes, representing about 20 percent of the total electoral votes a presidential *candidate* needs to win. A candidate might need to win several other states to equal the number of electoral votes in California alone if another candidate won in California.

In electoral college voting, a candidate is *awarded* a state's electoral votes if that candidate wins the popular vote in that state. The total of all the states' electoral votes equals 538. A candidate must receive at least 270, or one more than half of all the electoral votes, to win the election.

众议员，众议员人数视该州的人口来定。所以人口越多这个州的选票也就越多。

例如加利福尼亚州有55票，占总选票数的20%。若一候选人在加州获胜，就会获得加州的全部选票。那么，其他候选人要想获胜，可能就要获得其他几个州的全部选票。

选举团选举中，赢得最多普选票的候选人往往也会赢得多数的选举团票。全美各州的选票一共538张。候选人要赢得选举，必须赢得至少270张的选票。

---

representative *n.* 代表；众议院议员
candidate *n.* 候选人

electoral *adj.* 选举人的；竞选者的
award *v.* 授予；给予

Only four times in U.S. history has the winner of the electoral college not won the popular vote *nationwide*. In 2000 the election was very *close*. Before Florida's vote was decided, Bush had a total of 246 electoral college votes, and Gore had 266. Both candidates needed Florida's electoral college votes to win. After Florida's voting results were *sorted out*, the state's electoral votes went to George Bush. That brought his total to 271 electoral votes, and he became the 43rd president of the United States.

　　美国历史上只有四位总统虽然未能赢得比对手更多的普选票，却因为赢得了更多的选举团票而当选总统。2000年大选候选人的票数十分接近，佛罗里达州投票之前布什的选举人票有246张，戈登有266票。他们都需要赢得佛罗里达州的选票。结果公布后，这个州选举人选票投给了乔治·布什，这为他赢得了共271张选票，因此当选为第43届美国总统。

---

nationwide *adv.* 全国性地　　　　　　　close *adj.* 接近的；势均力敌的
sort out 理顺；整理

38

Examining Election Results

Once an election is *over* and all of the votes are counted, it is interesting to look at some of the numbers that *shaped* the election. In the 2000 U.S. presidential election, 105,405,100 people voted. This number represents 67 percent of the 156,421,000 people who were *registered* to vote. That means 33 percent of the people

425 416

选举结果的检测

选举结束，统计选票时，看着那些决定选举结果的数字真是有趣。2000年美国总统大选时，登记投票人数为156 421 000，但有105 405 100人投了票，占总人数的67%，也就是说有33%的选民放

---

over *adj.* 已完结的；已结束的

register *v.* 登记；注册

shape *v.* 决定……的形成；影响

who *signed up* to vote did not *cast* their vote.

In 2000 the number of people old enough to vote was 213,954,023. But only 49 percent of these voters did vote (105405100 ÷ 213954023 = 0.49). In other words, of the total number of people *eligible* to vote, more than half did not.

How does that percentage compare to other countries? In the United Kingdom, 71 percent of people registered to vote took part in the 1997 election. That represented 69 percent of all the people eligible to vote that year. In the Russian elections in 1999, 60 percent of people who registered voted, which was 59 percent of the people eligible. Using calculations, we can turn *raw* numbers about voting into a sense of who and how many people do vote. But the reason why so many do not vote goes beyond the power of numbers to explain.

弃了投票。

2000年，具有投票资格的人数为213 954 023，但只有49%的人投票（105 405 100÷213 954 023=0.49）。换句话说，有超过半数的合法选民放弃了投票。

与其他国家相比，这一比率如何呢？1997年英国大选有71%的人登记投票，占可投票人数的69%。1999年俄罗斯大选有60%的注册选民投了票，占可投票人数的59%。经计算就可以知道大致上哪些人、多少人参与投票。单从数据上还解释不了未投票的原因。

---

sign up 报名；登记

eligible *adj.* 有资格的；具备条件的

cast *v.* 登记（票数）；投（票）

raw *adj.* 未经分析或处理的

39

Vietnamese Americans: An American Success Story

The families of many Vietnamese Americans arrived in the United States beginning in the 1960s and continuing through the 1980s. Many came here *because of* war. All of them were looking for a better life. Today, more than one million Vietnamese Americans live in the United States. Their story is a success

美国成功故事：越裔美国人

从 20世纪60年代到80年代，许多越裔家庭进入美国。许多人来到这里是为了躲避战争，追求更好的生活。如今，生活在美国的越裔美国人已有一百多万。我们可通过统计学来研究他们的成功故事。

---

because of 因为；由于

story that we can study through *statistics*.

Statistics is a branch of mathematics. It uses numbers to look at "little pictures" of the world we live in to understand its "big pictures." Using statistics, we can learn *a great deal* about the Vietnamese Americans' experience in this country.

A *study* done in California in the year 2000 reported that most Vietnamese Americans live in California. Texas has the second-largest number of Vietnamese Americans, with large communities in Houston, Dallas, and Austin. The state of Washington has the third most.

Statistics also showed that 11 percent of all Vietnamese Americans are *self-employed*. The study suggested that as many as 99 percent of these business owners are first-generation Americans. First-generation means these people were born in Vietnam and moved

---

统计学是数学的一个分支。它利用数据从生活的"小视野"来理解其蕴含的"大道理"。通过统计学，我们从这个国家的越裔美国人经历中获益匪浅。

2000年，加利福尼亚州的一项调查表明，多数越裔美国人居住在加利福尼亚州。德克萨斯州的越裔美国人口数位列第二，其中大多数居住在休斯顿、达拉斯、奥斯汀。华盛顿州则位列第三。

数据还显示11%的越裔美国人从事个体工商业。研究表明，高达99%的商人是第一代美国人（移民）。这里"第一代"是指那些出生在越南后

---

statistics *n.* 统计学；统计数字
study *n.* 研究；调查

to the United States. This group faced two big problems when they came to America. First of all, they could not speak English. And, like many other *immigrant* groups, they also faced *prejudice*. There were few jobs they could do, and most jobs paid low wages. Starting their own business gave them a better chance for success.

The same study reported that about 64 percent of the businesses started by Vietnamese Americans are in the service industry. These businesses include beauty shops and *barbershops*, *laundries*, and health care clinics. Another 24 percent of the businesses are retail businesses, such as restaurants, grocery stores, and small shops. Half of the businesses claim that more than 75 percent of their customers are "ethnic customers". In this case, ethnic is likely to mean "mostly Vietnamese American".

These numbers tell us that most opportunities for first-generation

移居美国的人。这些人一到美国就面临两大问题。首先是他们不会说英语。再者，和其他移民团体一样，要面临歧视问题。提供给他们的工作很少，而且多数工作薪水很低。创业为他们的成功提供了更好的机会。

研究还表明，服务行业中约有64%的公司是由越裔美国人创建的。这些企业包括美容院、理发店、洗衣店和小诊所。另有24%的公司从事零售业。例如餐厅、食杂店和一些小店。半数的商店声称超过75%的顾客都是"同族顾客"。这里"同族"是指几乎都是越裔美国人。

这些数据说明，第一代越裔移民者的多数机会就在本群体中。二、三代越裔美国人中这一数据有所不同。为什么？也许是因为在美国，人们认

immigrant n.（自国外移入的）移民　　　　prejudice n. 偏见；歧视
barbershop n. 理发店　　　　　　　　　　laundry n. 洗衣店；洗衣房

Vietnamese immigrants lay within their own *communities*. The statistics are different for second- and third-generation Vietnamese Americans. Why? Perhaps because hard work and education are the keys to success in the United States. Vietnamese American adults worked hard to make sure their children could get a better education than theirs. They made sure their children worked hard at school so they could go to college. Statistics *suggest* that Vietnamese Americans are an American success story.

为努力工作和教育是成功的关键。成年越裔美国人努力工作，使他们的孩子获得更好的教育，并为他们的孩子能在学校努力学习，考上大学提供保障。数据显示越裔美国人是美国成功的故事。

---

community *n.* 团体；界；群体　　　　　　　　　suggest *v.* 表明；使认为

40

Vietnamese Americans Have Two Birthdays

Can you be 10 years old and 11 years old at the same time? You can if you are Vietnamese American. In the United States, your birthday is the day you were born. For many Vietnamese, however, it doesn't *matter* what day you were born on, because everyone's birthday is *celebrated* on Tet.

越裔美国人有两个生日

你能同时10岁和11岁吗？如果你是越裔美国人就可以。在美国，生日是指你出生的那天。对于许多越南人来说，哪天出生并不重要，因为每个人都在Tet(越南春节)时庆祝生日。

---

matter *v.* 重要；要紧

celebrate *v.* 庆祝；祝贺

Tet is the festival that welcomes the lunar new year. In Vietnam, the *calendar* follows the movements of the moon and not the sun. Tet begins with the first moon of the year. On the *solar* calendar, used in the United States, Tet usually falls between January 21 and February 19.

Tet marks the arrival of spring. It's a time for a fresh beginning and high hopes. It's also a time for presents, and children receive "lucky money" *tucked* into red *envelopes*. And everyone turns one year older on the first day of the new year.

In 2004 Tet fell on Thursday, January 22. Consider this: If you had been born on January 22, 2003, you would have been exactly one year old on January 22, 2004, according to either the lunar or the solar calendar. If you had been born on July 22, 2003, you would have been six months old under the solar calendar but celebrating your first "birthday" under the Vietnamese calendar.

　　Tet是迎接阴历新年的节日。在越南，历法依据的是月球的运动而非太阳的运动。新年是从每年的第一次月出开始的。美国使用的阳历中，新年通常在1月21日到2月19日。

　　春节标志着春天的到来。这是树立新起点与希望的时候，也是交换礼物的时候。孩子们会收到装在红包里的"压岁钱"。新年的第一天每个人都长了一岁。

　　2004年的春节是1月22日，星期四。想一下，如果你在2003年1月22日出生，那么无论是根据阴历还是阳历，2004年1月22日这一天你都一岁了。若你在2003年7月22日出生，那么根据阳历，你就6个月大，而根据越南历法，你在这时则庆祝一岁的生日。

---

calendar *n.* 历法；日历　　　　　　　　solar *adj.* 太阳的

tuck *v.* 塞进；折叠　　　　　　　　　　envelope *n.* 信封；封皮

41

Counting in American Indian Beadwork

People have been making things with *beads* for thousands of years. One of the oldest beads found is more than 10,000 years old. Beads were often used to *embellish craftwork* and clothing. Embellish means to *decorate* or improve something by adding detail. American Indians have a long history of working with beads. They have

美印第安镶珠工艺中的计数

人们利用珠子制作饰品已有数千年的历史。人们发现的最早的珠饰至今已有一万多年了。人们经常用珠子来装饰工艺品和服饰。点缀是用添加小物件来装饰或美化某一物品。美印第安人用珠子加工产品已有很久的历史了。他们利用各种不同的天然材料，如贝壳、石头、

---

bead *n.* 珠子；有孔的小珠
craftwork *n.* 工艺品

embellish *v.* 美化；装饰
decorate *v.* 装饰；装点

been making beads from many different natural materials, such as shells, stones, *gems*, *ivory*, clay, seeds, wood, and bone.

Beadwork is a combination of types and patterns of beads that make up a colorful design. Beads are strung on string and "woven" together to create what looks very much like *fabric*. American Indian craftspeople counted beads so that several different sizes could be used together to make patterns for beadwork. The patterns were often *geometric* shapes, but sometimes they represented things found in nature.

Modern craftspeople use manufactured beads made of glass and plastic as well as natural stone and wood. The beads are numbered to show their different sizes. Tiny beads are size 22/0. This means that 22 of these beads will fit on one inch of string. Larger beads are

---

宝石、象牙、黏土、种子、木材、骨头等加工珠子。

　　镶珠工艺是将各式珠饰混合制成色彩鲜明的图案。他们将珠子串在细绳上，并将其编织成类似布的产品。美印第安工匠数珠子数目，这样做以便大小不同的珠子串在一起形成不同的图案。镶珠的图案通常都是地理图形，但有时也会展现自然事物。

　　现代工匠既使用天然的石珠和木珠，也使用玻璃或塑料制成的人工镶珠。将镶珠编码，以代表不同的规格、尺寸。小珠的规格为22/0，即每英寸的线串有22个这样的珠子。大珠的规格为6/0，即每英寸串有6个这样的珠子。

---

gem *n.* 宝石　　　　　　　　　　　ivory *n.* 象牙
fabric *n.* 织物；布　　　　　　　　geometric *adj.* 几何图形的

size 6/0, meaning six beads per inch.

Think about making a piece of *beadwork* that is 12 inches square. First, you would imagine your design. Then you would decide the color and size of the beads. Finally, you would figure out how many beads are needed.

For this example, the design will *comprise* six two-inch *bands*, or *stripes*, of equal width and various colors. The beads will be of six different sizes: 20/0 white beads, 15/0 black beads, 12/0 green beads, 10/0 yellow beads, 8/0 blue beads, and 6/0 red beads. Remember, the piece is 12 inches by 12 inches, so each of the 6 stripes is 2 inches wide and 12 inches long. And each of the stripes will be made with one of these types of beads.

To find how many beads you require, look at how many beads will

---

　　思考如何制作一个12平方英寸的珠工艺品。首先构思一下你的设计，再决定珠子的颜色和大小，最后计算出所需珠子数量。

　　例如，这一设计有6条等宽而颜色各异的2寸带子或条纹。这需要采用6种规格的珠子：20/0的白珠，15/0的黑珠，12/0的绿珠，10/0的黄珠，8/0的蓝珠，以及6/0的红珠。记住珠饰的尺寸是12英寸×12英寸，因此需要6部分共同组成，每块长12英寸、宽2英寸。并且每一块采用一种类型的珠子。

　　为算出所需珠子的数目，那就要看每英寸所需珠子的数目。一英寸要20个白珠，那么它的宽就用20乘以2，长用20乘以12来计算。然后将两个

---

beadwork *n.* 珠饰品　　　　　　　comprise *v.* 包括；包含
band *n.* 带；箍　　　　　　　　　stripe *n.* 条纹；线条

cover one inch. There are 20 white beads to one inch. So *multiply* 20 by 2 for the *width* and 20 by 12 for the length. Then multiply these two *products* (20 × 2 = 40; 20 × 12 = 240; 240 × 40 = 9, 600). You need 9,600 white beads. Using the same *formula*, you find that you need 5,400 black beads and 3,456 green beads. You also need 2,400 yellow beads, 1,536 blue beads, and 864 red beads. For your piece of beadwork you'll need a total of 23,256 beads.

结果相乘（20×2=40；20×12=240；240×40=9 600）得出需要9 600个白珠。同理，算得需要5 400个黑珠，3 456个绿珠，2 400个黄珠，1 536个蓝珠和864个红珠。所以，完成整件镶珠工艺品总共需要23 256个珠子。

---

multiply *v.* 乘；相乘
product *n.* 乘积；结果

width *n.* 宽度
formula *n.* 公式；方程式

42

Counting on a Chinese Abacus

An *abacus* has beads that *slide* on wooden rods. The ancient Chinese used the abacus to count, add, and subtract. An abacus has a *rectangular* frame. Parallel *vertical* rods run across the abacus. The rod farthest right stands for the ones place. The next rod to the left is the tens place, the next the hundreds place, and so

中国算盘中的计数

算盘的细杆上串有算盘珠，古代中国使用算盘来进行计数，加法和减法。算盘为矩形木框，其内纵向排列细杆，杆上串有算珠。右侧最远的细杆代表个位，其左侧相邻杆为十位，接下来是百位，以

abacus *n.* 算盘
rectangular *adj.* 长方形的；矩形的

slide *v.* 滑动；滑行
vertical *adj.* 竖的；垂直的

on. A *beam* runs across the rods and *divides* them into a lower deck and an upper *deck*. On each rod, there are five beads on the lower deck and two on the upper. Each bead on the bottom stands for one unit of that rod's *place value*. Each bead on the top is five units of the place value. To count, beads are moved toward the beam.

Here's how to count 268 on an abacus. On the ones rod, move three lower beads up to the beam and one upper bead down to the beam—3 + 5 = 8. On the tens rod, move one lower bead up and one upper bead down—10 + 50 = 60. On the hundreds rod, move two lower beads up—200. Now add up the three values—200 + 60 + 8 = 268.

此类推。横梁穿过细杆把算珠分为上下两部分。每根细杆，梁上两珠，每珠作数五，梁下五珠，每珠作数一。向横梁方向拨动算珠来进行运算。

　　这里向大家展示如何用算盘表示268。个位上，梁下拨三珠，梁上拨一珠，即3+5=8；十位上，梁下拨一珠，梁上拨一珠，即10+50=60；百位上，梁下拨两珠，即200。将三个数值相加即200+60+8=268。

---

beam *n.* 梁   divide *v.* 分开；分隔

deck *n.* 一层；层面   place value 位值

43

Adding & Multiplying: Related Methods

Mario's uncle, Tio Manuel, was replacing the old *tile* in a restaurant with new tile. The new tile would be the same size as the old tile, so they would need the same number of tiles. Tio Manuel asked Mario to figure out how many tiles they would need for the floor. Mario began to count the tiles. But the restaurant was

两大相关运算：加法与乘法

马里奥的叔叔蒂奥·马缪尔准备为餐厅更换新的瓷砖。由于新旧瓷砖尺寸一致，因此需要的瓷砖数目也一样。蒂奥·马缪尔让马里奥算一下铺地所需的瓷砖数目。马里奥开始数瓷砖，但餐厅太大，他

tile *n.* 瓷砖；花砖；地砖

very large, and he kept losing count.

Mario needed a better method. He realized that each row contained 24.5 tiles, so he *rounded* the figure up to 25 to make his calculations easier. That would allow him to *estimate* the number of tiles needed. Mario wrote 25 + 25 + 25, and so on. For each of 20 rows of tile, Mario wrote down another 25. When he was finished, he solved the *addition*. He determined they would need 500 tiles.

When Tio Manuel saw the figure, he looked at the floor and began to count the number of tiles in a row and then the number of rows. Tio Manuel multiplied 25 times 20, and he, too, found that they needed 500 tiles. He praised Mario for his math skills. Mario was surprised, however, that he and his uncle had arrived at the same answer. He had found the sum of the tiles through addition, but his

---

总是数错。

　　马里奥需要一个更好的方法。他发现每列有24.5块砖，因此为方便计算，他取其近似值25计算瓷砖数。这样，每列25块，共20列。为估算出瓷砖数目，马里奥列出算式 25+25+25……，相加计算得出要用500块瓷砖。

　　蒂奥·马缪尔看了看结果，又看了看地面，数了一排的瓷砖数及排数。然后他用25乘以20，也得出要用500块。他称赞了马里奥的运算能力。马里奥感到非常吃惊，他用加法，而叔叔用乘法，竟然得出同样的结

---

round *v.* 使凑整；四舍五入　　　　　　estimate *v.* 估计；估算
addition *n.* 加；加法

uncle had used *multiplication*. Tio Manuel explained that Mario had added 25 a total of 20 times, which was the same as multiplying 25 by 20.

Mario decided to try to use multiplication too. He counted the number of tiles in one row along the side wall first, and then he counted the number of rows. He counted 20 tiles and 25 rows. Mario wrote 20 times 25 and solved the multiplication. He was *astonished* when his answer was again 500, because his calculation looked different from his uncle's. Why did 25 times 20 and 20 times 25 yield the same answer?

Tio Manuel explained that rearranging the *factors* (the numbers multiplied) didn't change the product (the multiplication result). He showed Mario that the same *law* applied to addition. He counted the

---

果。蒂奥·马缪尔解释道20个25相加和25乘以20是一样的。

马里奥决定也用乘法试试。先数好靠墙那排的瓷砖数，再数了排数，知道了每排20块，一共25排。用20块乘以25排，即20×25，看到他算得的结果仍为500块时他感到很惊讶，因为他的算法似乎和叔叔的不一样。为什么25×20和20×25会得到同样的答案呢？

蒂奥·马缪尔向他解释道，交换因子（乘数）不会改变计算结果（乘积）。且这一法则同样适用于加法。接着他数了靠墙那排的瓷砖数又数了另一边的，计算20+25和25+20，得到的总和均为45。改变加数（相加

---

multiplication *n.* 乘法；乘法运算
factor *n.* 因子；因数

astonished *adj.* 感到十分惊讶的；吃惊的
law *n.* 规律；法则

tile along one wall and then along the other. He showed that 20 plus 25 and 25 plus 20 yielded the same sum: 45. Changing the order of the addends (the numbers that are added) did not affect the sum (the addition result). This is because both addition and multiplication are bound by the *commutative* law.

数）位置不会影响总和（相加结果）。这是因为加法和乘法都是按"交换律"进行运算的。

commutative *adj.* 交换的

44

Tiling the Kitchen Counter

Jean wanted to buy new tiles for her kitchen *countertop*. The counter is 24 inches wide by 96 inches long. Jean decided to use four-inch-square blue-and-white tiles, which she would put down in a *checkerboard pattern*. Using division, Jean found she needed six rows of 24 tiles each. Jean multiplied 6 times 24 to find the total

给厨房台面贴砖

简想为厨房台面购置新砖。这个台面长96英寸，宽24英寸。简决定用4平方英寸的蓝白砖铺成象棋棋盘图案。她用除法计算后发现需要6排瓷砖，每排24块，6×24后得出共需144块砖。她想把花销控制在200美元以内。于是她把每块砖的预算限定为1美元，即总价144美

countertop *n.* （尤指厨房的）操作台　　checkerboard *n.* 棋盘；棋盘状（物）
pattern *n.* 图案；花样

number of tiles she needed: 144. Jean did not want to spend more than $200 on the project. She *set* a spending *limit* of $1 for each tile, or a total of $144. This way, Jean would be sure to have enough money left in her budget to buy other supplies and some tools.

The tile store had the perfect tiles on sale. They were being sold in boxes of 25 for $19 a box. Jean knew that she needed to buy six boxes of tiles. So she multiplied 6 times $19 to find the amount of money she would spend, getting a total of $114. She had *originally* decided she could afford to spend $144 on tiles, so she was well within her budget. Perhaps she could tile the back of the counter too. Jean went home to measure the area to see whether she could tile it and still stay within her budget.

元。这样她就有足够的钱来采买其他用品及工具。

瓷砖店正好出售上等的瓷砖。以箱出售，售价为19美元，共25块。简需要买6箱，用6×19得出总价为114美元。她原本打算花144美元买砖，所以这个价钱刚好在她的预算之内。也许她能连同台面后侧也铺上瓷砖。简回家去测一下面积看看能否在不超预算的前提下，把台后也贴上瓷砖。

---

set *v.* 设置；确定　　　　　　　　　　　　　　　　　limit *n.* 限制；界限
originally *adv.* 起初；本来

45

Worldwide Time Zones

P*rior to* the late 19th century, each town did its own *timekeeping*. In some places, it was up to the clockmaker to keep the town clock set *accurately*. The clockmaker would *observe* when the sun reached its highest point in the sky and then set the clock to noon. Setting the time this way meant that the time was slightly

世界时区

19世纪末以前，每个城镇都有自己的计时方法。一些地区由钟表匠设定标准时间。钟表匠会观察太阳，当太阳升至最高点时，他们就把钟表调至中午12时。这种设置时间的方式意味着这一地区的各城镇

---

prior to 在……之前
accurately *adv.* 准确地；精确地

timekeeping *n.* 计时
observe *v.* 仔细观察；观测

different in every town in the area.

When railroads came to the United States, train schedules were confusing. Each stop was based on the time in that town. People needed a way of keeping time that was *consistent* wherever they traveled.

In 1878 a Canadian, Sir Sandford Fleming, suggested that the world be divided into 24 time zones, each one 15 degrees of *longitude* wide. Longitudes are *imaginary* lines around Earth that pass through the North and South Poles.

In 1884 people from many countries met and found a way of making rules for setting time around the world. The line of longitude that passes through Greenwich, England, was set as the zero point of longitude—0 degrees. It was called the *prime meridian*. All other time zones in the world were measured from this point. That means

---

时间上会有细微不同。

火车进入美国时，火车时刻表让人费解。每站都以当地时间为准，然而人们需要的是无论走到哪里时间都能保持一致。

1878年，加拿大人桑福德·弗莱明爵士建议将世界划分为24个时区，每个时区跨15个经度。经度是指地球上连接南北极的虚拟线。

1884年，来自不同国家的人聚在一起商定了设定世界时间的方法。人们将穿过英格兰格林尼治的经线定为零度经线，被称作本初子午线。世界上其他所有时区均以这条经线为标准，即本初子午线以西，每个时区提

---

consistent *adj.* 一贯的；始终如一的
imaginary *adj.* 假想的；虚构的

longitude *n.* 经度
prime meridian 本初子午线

that, moving west from the prime meridian, each time zone is one hour earlier. Moving east, each time zone is one hour later.

Today all countries follow the system, but some countries have made changes to it. China is so large that it is in five time zones. However, the Chinese government decided to use only one zone so that all Chinese *citizens* would be on the same time. Russia has 11 time zones, but 10 of them are one hour ahead of the time they should follow according to their distance from Greenwich.

In the United States, Congress *standardized* the time zones in 1918. The time zone lines were drawn to avoid *populated* areas, so the lines are not straight. All together, there are nine time zones for the United States and its territories. These zones are (from east to west) the Eastern, Central, Mountain, Pacific, Alaska, Hawaii-Aleutian, Samoan, Wake Island, and Guam time zones. This means, then,

---

前一个小时，向东每时区推迟一个小时。

现在所有国家均采用这一划分方法，但也有一些国家稍有变动。中国幅员辽阔，横跨5个时区。中国政府决定只采用一个时区，这样全体公民就生活在同一时间。俄罗斯跨越11个时区，但根据它距格林尼治的实际距离所推算的时间，其中有10个时区的时间要提前一个小时。

1918年，美国国会确立了时区划分标准。时区划分时避开了人们的活动区域，因此，时区线不是直线。美国领土共分为9个时区，自东向西依次是东部时间、中央时间，山脉时间、太平洋时间、阿拉斯加时间、夏

---

citizen *n.* 公民；市民   standardize *v.* 使标准化；按标准校准
populated *adj.* 有人居住的

that at 9 P.M. in New York City, it is 12 noon on the island of Guam (9 P.M. − 9 hours = 0, or noon). Each year many states adjust their time zones to *daylight* saving time, moving one hour ahead in April. Then they go back to standard time in October.

威夷一阿留申时间、萨摩亚时间、威克岛时间、关岛时间。也就是说如果纽约是晚上9点，那么关岛就是中午12点（下午9点−9小时=0点/中午）。每年都会有很多州为获得日照时间而调整时区，四月份提前一小时，十月份再调整回标准时间。

daylight *n.* 日光；白昼

46

Traveling Through Time Zones

Paul had to *depart* for Vienna, Austria, on business. His plans were to leave Minneapolis, which is in the Central Time Zone of the United States, at 11 A.M. on Tuesday. He knew that for every new time zone he *traversed* on his way east, the time would be one hour later. The flight would be 16 hours long.

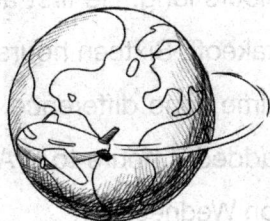

跨时区旅行

保罗去奥地利的维也纳出差，计划于星期二上午11点抵达位于美国中央时区的明尼波利斯。据他所知，每向东一时区，时间就向后一小时，这次航班共飞行16个小时。

depart *v.* 启程前往……；离开　　　　　　traverse *v.* 穿越；横跨

He flew east across the United States and across the Atlantic Ocean. His plane landed in London, which is six time zones east of Minneapolis. From there he got on another plane and flew one more time zone to the east. He landed in Vienna at 10 A.M. on Wednesday. He took a short *nap*, showered, and ate a late breakfast. He arrived at his meeting at 1 P.M.

Paul wasn't sure the *airline* had given him the correct *arrival* time. So he checked, using a little math. He knew that the *flight* was 16 hours long. He first added the 16 hours of flight time to his 11 A.M. takeoff. Sixteen hours after 11 A.M. is 3 A.M. Then he calculated the time zone difference. He flew east across seven time zones, so he added 7 hours to 3 A.M. and found that he would arrive at 10 A.M. on Wednesday.

他的航班穿越美国向东飞行，横跨大西洋，然后降落在明尼波利斯以东6个时区的伦敦。从这里他搭乘另一航班再向东飞行一个时区。星期三早上十点降落在维也纳。他小睡了一会，沐浴用餐后，于下午1点抵达会场。

保罗不确定航空公司给出的抵达时间是否正确。因此，他用数学知识核查了一下。他共飞行16个小时。出发时间是上午11点，再加上16个小时飞行的时间，就应该是凌晨3点。接着计算时差，他向东跨越了7个时区，在凌晨3点加上7个小时，计算出他于星期三上午10点到达目的地。

---

nap *n.* 小睡；打盹
arrival *n.* 到达；抵达

airline *n.* 航空公司
flight *n.* 飞行；航班

47

Statistics

Statistics is a type of *applied* mathematics that helps us make calculated *guesses* when we don't have all the information. Doctors *seeking* the best *cure* may use statistics. They treat a group of people with a new medicine, count how many of these people got better, and calculate what percentage got better. Then

统计学

统计学是一种应用数学，旨在帮助我们在尚未完全获得信息时进行推测猜想。医生可能利用统计学寻找最好的治疗方案。他们运用新药治疗病人，计算好转人数，并计算其百分比。然后与其他治疗方

---

applied *adj.* 应用的；实用的
seek *v.* 寻找；寻求

guess *n.* 猜想；推测
cure *n.* 药物；疗法

they compare this percentage to percentages from other treatments, using statistics formulas and *charts* to decide which medicine is better.

Engineers who plan street systems often use statistics to help create the best designs for future traffic *flow*. To find out whether changes need to be made to the design of streets, engineers look at how many people live in the area and how many people use the area streets. They would also have to find out whether these numbers are likely to stay the same or whether they may change. An increase in drivers might mean that engineers would have to improve the design of area streets.

For example, statistics show that the population of drivers in Maytown in 1970 was 30,400. By 1980 the population of drivers had risen to 33,500. This was *roughly* a 10 percent increase over 10

案的好转人数百分比进行对比，并运用统计学公式及图表来确定哪种药物更有效。

工程师在规划道路系统时，常运用统计学知识来设计最佳方案。在考虑是否对街道设计进行修改时，工程师需观察这一地区的常住人口以及使用此地区道路的人数，还要查明上述数据是保持不变还是可能有所变动。若司机人数增加，工程师则要改善区域道路的规划。

例如，统计显示1970年梅敦的司机人数是30 400人，到1980年司机人数增长到33 500人，10年间约增长了10%（33 500 − 30 400=3 100；

---

chart *n.* 图表　　　　　　　　　　　flow *n.* 流动；流量
roughly *adv.* 大致地；粗略地

years (33,500 − 30,400 = 3,100; 3,100 ÷ 30,400 = 0.10). In 1990 the driving population was 36,900, and in 2000 it was 41,000. So the increase in driving population had remained *constant* at about 10 percent every 10 years. During the same years, the job market, which brought new people to Maytown, had grown at a *steady* rate. This meant that the percentage increase in population would likely remain steady.

The engineers wanted their streets to *handle* the traffic flow smoothly through the year 2030. On the basis of this statistical analysis, the engineers felt sure in planning for a 10 percent increase in drivers for each 10-year period from 2000 through 2030.

Statistics also can be used for choosing the best product. Let's say you wanted to find the longest-lasting *batteries* for a handheld ame. You visit several Web sites. Each of these sites give results from battery tests. But these results do not completely agree. The

---

3 100÷30 400=0.10）。1990年司机人数为36 900，2000年为41 000，因此每10年司机人数仍维持大概10%的增长率。同期，招聘外来人员的数目也平稳增长。也就是人口增长率保持稳定。

工程师希望他们设计的道路到2030年仍能保持交通顺畅。在统计分析基础上，工程师们在规划时可以确保2000年至2030年间每10年司机人数的增长率为10%。

统计学也应用于选择最佳产品。假设要为掌上游戏机配最耐用的电池，你会浏览许多网站。每个网站都会提供电池测试结果，而这些结果却

---

constant *adj.* 不变的；固定的
handle *v.* 处理；应付

steady *adj.* 稳定的；平稳的
battery *n.* 电池

difference in results might have been caused by the different ways the tests were run. In this *case*, taking an average of the test results will give you a result you can use. Statistics is a mathematical tool that helps us make good decisions.

不尽相同。测试方法不同，可能导致其结果不同。在这种情况下，你就可以采用此结果的平均值。统计学是帮助我们作出明智决定的一种数学工具。

---

case *n.* 情况；情形

48

Newspaper Circulation and Revenue

Newspaper companies make money in two ways: by selling papers and by selling *advertising* space. *Circulation* is the total number of *copies* a newspaper sells each day. Earnings from newspaper sales make up about 18 percent of most newspapers' total *revenue*—the money that the company makes. The rest comes from

报纸的发行量与收益

报社通过两种方式赚钱：一种是销售报纸，另一种是销售广告版面。发行量是指报纸的日销售总量。对于大部分报社来说，报纸销售额约占总收益的18%，这里总收益是指报纸总收入。其余的收入来

---

advertise *v.* 做广告；登广告
copy *n.* （出版物的）（一）本；（一）份

circulation *n.* 流通；发行（量）
revenue *n.* 收入；总收入

advertising.

Besides its own circulation, a newspaper must look at its market *share*. Market share for a daily city newspaper has to do with the company's newspaper sales *compared* to the sales of other daily newspaper companies in that city. Market share also shows how much of the total money spent on newspaper advertising in a city goes to each newspaper.

Advertising market share is expressed as a percentage. For example, the *Boston Globe* holds an 85 percent share of newspaper advertising revenue in Boston. This means that 85 percent of all the newspaper advertising bought in Boston is in the *Globe*.

The greater the circulation a newspaper has, the more it can charge for advertising. An advertiser pays for ad space in a

---

自广告费。

　　除了发行量，报社也要关注报纸所占的市场份额。城市日报的市场份额与同城其他同类日报销售量有关。市场份额还显示出这个城市里每种报纸的广告开销情况。

　　广告的市场份额是以百分数的形式表达。例如，《波士顿环球时报》占波士顿总广告收益的85%。也就是说，在波士顿，85%的报纸广告来自《环球时报》。

　　报纸的发行量越大，其广告费也越高。广告商所付的版面费由该报的读者数目决定。若报纸有很大的发行量，就意味着很多读者会在该报看到

---

share *n.* 份额；分担量　　　　　　　　　　　　compare *v.* 比较；对照

newspaper on the basis of the number of people who read the paper. If a newspaper has a large circulation, that means many *readers* are seeing the advertising in the paper. That newspaper can *charge* more for advertising space than a paper with a smaller circulation can. Even so, sometimes the advertiser can get a better *deal* by paying more for ad space.

Here's an example. *Daily Times* has a circulation of 25,000 readers. It charges $1,500 for a quarter-page ad. The *Gazette* has a circulation of 35,000. It charges $1,750 for a quarter page. But the *Gazette* is the better value because it is read by more people. The *proof* is in the math. By dividing the cost of the ad by the number of readers, the advertiser can find out the cost per reader. The *Times* charges $.06 per reader ($1,500 ÷ 25,000 = $0.06). The *Gazette*

广告。这家报社就可以比发行量较小的报社赚更多的广告费。即使如此，有时广告商支付较多的广告费能获得更大收益。

比如说，《每日时报》拥有25 000份的发行量，1/4版的广告要价1 500美元。《菲尼克斯报》的发行量为35 000份，所以1/4版的广告要价1 750美元。《菲尼克斯报》价值更高，因为它拥有更多的读者。用数学就可以证明。用广告费除以读者数就得出每份报纸的成本。《每日时报》的成本为每份0.06美元（1 500美元÷25 000=0.06美元）。《菲尼克斯报》每份0.05美元（1 750美元÷35 000=0.05美元）。即使《菲尼克斯报》1/4的版面费更贵，但平均到每位读者，广告商就花得相对较少。

---

reader *n.* 读者
deal *n.* 交易；生意

charge *v.* 要价；收费
proof *n.* 证据；证明

charges $.05 per reader ($1,750 ÷ 35,000 = $0.05). Even though a quarter-page ad costs more in the *Gazette*, the advertiser is paying less per reader.

Newspapers try to find out the kinds of things that readers like or don't like in a newspaper. From its *findings*, the newspaper can make changes to the paper to help increase circulation. By increasing circulation, the newspaper earns more money by selling more papers. It can also charge more for advertising space. Increasing circulation is a "can't lose" situation.

报社极其关注读者的喜好，并据此作出调整以获得更大的发行量。发行量增大，报社就会卖出更多的报纸并且获利更多，广告费也就随之而提高了。增大发行量是个"稳赢不输"的策略。

---

finding *n.* 结论；结果

49

Managing a Neighborhood Newspaper

Salena is the *editor* of the *Hometown Herald*. She must make sure the paper earns a *profit* after all its monthly expenses. Salena pays $400 each week to *employees*. Each week the *Herald* spends $345 to print the newspapers.

To calculate her monthly costs, Salena first multiplied $400 by 4 to find that employee

社区报纸的管理

赛琳娜是《故乡先驱报》的编辑。她要保证报社每月除去开销后有所盈利。赛琳娜每周要支付给员工400美元。《先驱报》每周要花费345美元印刷报纸。

为计算月开支，赛琳娜先用400美元乘以4得到每月工资费用为1 600

editor *n.* 编辑；校订者
employee *n.* 雇员；职员

profit *n.* 收益；利润

costs are $1,600 a month. She calculated the monthly *printing* costs as $1,380. The paper rents offices for $400 a month. So total monthly costs are $3,380.

One way a newspaper makes money is circulation, or sales. Salena sells an average of 1,886 papers a month. Readers pay 50 cents for a paper. To calculate the paper's total circulation revenue, Salena multiplied 50 cents by 1,886, which equals $943 in monthly sales.

Andrew sells advertisement space in the *Hometown Herald*. A newspaper page is divided into *columns*, which are measured in inches. Advertisers pay the newspaper by the number of inches of column space they need for the ad. On average, the paper makes $2,700 a month from advertising sales.

美元，印刷费为每月1 380美元，办公室租金为每月400美元。因此，每月共支出3 380美元。

　　发行量即销售额是报社收入的一种。赛琳娜平均每月卖出1 886份报纸，每份50美分。为计算总发行收入，赛琳娜用50美分乘以1 886得出每月报纸的销售额为943美元。

　　安德鲁负责《故乡先驱报》广告版面的销售。一份报纸被分为不同专栏，专栏大小用英寸计算。广告商根据所需专栏大小来支付费用。报社平均每月广告销售额为2 700美元。

---

printing *n.* 印刷　　　　　　　　　　　　　　column *n.* 专栏；栏

Salena had determined that the *Herald's* monthly costs *totaled* $3,380. Newspaper sales of $943 and ad sales of $2,700 make the total revenue $3,643. Subtracting the total costs from the total revenue leaves a monthly profit of $263.

赛琳娜算出《先驱报》每月共支出3 380美元。报纸销售额为943美元，再加上广告销售额2 700美元，这样总收入为3 643美元。总收入减去总开支得出月利润为263美元。

---

total *v.* 总计；总数达

Salena had determined that the Herald's monthly costs totaled $3,380. Newspaper sales of $694? and ad sales of $2,100 make the total revenue $3,643. Subtracting the total costs from the total revenue leaves a monthly profit of $263.

桑坦德银行《金融报》管理分析师5 280美元。消费信贷管理员394美元

瓦、银行工作的年薪能达700美元。风投资C/35 649美元。私募入职后